Introductio

What makes a record deserve its own book? If it draws you in and tells something different with each approach. Every time you listen, you discover things you did not hear before but must have been there all along. Such a record is open to an ongoing dialogue. It is multi-layered and has many stories to tell. In a sense, the music itself asks to be described. From time to time, it calls the listener back. Most of all, a record that deserves its own book changes your listening perspective once and for all. It cannot be unheard. It extends beyond itself and influences how you listen to other music. The music crawls under your skin. For us, it turned out, writing about a single record meant writing about music as such.

This book tells the story of Einstürzende Neubauten's 1981 debut album *Kollaps*: ground-breaking and uncompromising music that remains as vital, exhilarating and surprising as the day it was released. Over the course of eight chapters, the book dissects this record from different perspectives. Each chapter stands as a short essay, focusing on a specific historical or theoretical theme.

The first two essays take the reader back to West-Berlin in the early 1980s. Walled off on all sides, the scarred half-city offered ideal circumstances for a fertile underground art scene to take shape. Einstürzende Neubauten emerged from these surroundings to make music that reflected the complexities of life in this Cold War city. As a result, their music expresses a strong sense of shared identity and a deep wish to belong.

This desire to belong and to connect is further explored in the next two essays. They deal, firstly, with Einstürzende Neubauten's riotous early live shows; and secondly, with different types of bodies that sound through in their work: in lyrical references, in the physicality of frontman Blixa Bargeld's voice and, more metaphorically, in the way the band challenged the organization of the body of music itself. On stage, the band members pushed their own body beyond its limits, and the palpable tension between structure and chaos that defines their music established a vital connection between the band and its audience. With this destructive approach to music-making, Einstürzende Neubauten took apart music and put it back together again in fresh and thrilling ways.

As discussed in the fifth and sixth essays, this continuous taking apart and putting back together was also key to the way the band handled the recording process. Exploring and subverting the artistic potential of music technology, they used experimental sound manipulation to achieve a similar visceral impact on record as they did on stage. On *Kollaps*, this is most apparent through all the bangs and crackling, cuts and feedback, static and drilling, shouts and whispers or, in short, through all the noises that invite the listener in.

The concluding essays extend upon this trope of reaching out to others by focusing on two guiding themes that underpin much of Einstürzende Neubauten's work: love and desire. Beyond all the racket and negativity, *Kollaps* is full of burning and sometimes destructive love for others, for each other and for music itself. On 'Sehnsucht', a song to which

Kollaps

33 1/3 Global

33 1/3 Global, a series related to but independent from **33 1/3**, takes the format of the original series of short, music-based books and brings the focus to music throughout the world. With initial volumes focusing on Japanese and Brazilian music, the series will also include volumes on the popular music of Australia/Oceania, Europe, Africa, the Middle East, and more.

33 1/3 Japan

Series Editor: Noriko Manabe

Spanning a range of artists and genres – from the 1970s rock of Happy End to technopop band Yellow Magic Orchestra, the Shibuya-kei of Cornelius, classic anime series *Cowboy Bebop*, J-Pop/EDM hybrid Perfume, and vocaloid star Hatsune Miku – **33 1/3 Japan** is a series devoted to in-depth examination of Japanese popular music of the twentieth and twenty-first centuries.

Published Titles:

Supercell's *Supercell* by Keisuke Yamada

AKB48 by Patrick W. Galbraith and Jason G. Karlin

Yoko Kanno's *Cowboy Bebop Soundtrack* by Rose Bridges

Perfume's *Game* by Patrick St. Michel

Cornelius's *Fantasma* by Martin Roberts

Joe Hisaishi's *My Neighbor Totoro: Soundtrack* by Kunio Hara

Shonen Knife's *Happy Hour* by Brooke McCorkle

Nenes' *Koza Dabasa* by Henry Johnson

Yuming's *The 14th Moon* by Lasse Lehtonen

Forthcoming Titles:

Yellow Magic Orchestra's *Yellow Magic Orchestra* by Toshiyuki Ohwada

Kohaku utagassen: The Red and White Song Contest by Shelley Brunt

Toshiko Akiyoshi-Lew Tabackin Big Band's *Kogun* by E. Taylor Atkins

S.O.B.'s *Don't Be Swindle* by Mahon Murphy and Ran Zwigenberg

33 1/3 Brazil

Series Editor: Jason Stanyek

Covering the genres of samba, tropicália, rock, hip hop, forró, bossa nova, heavy metal and funk, among others, **33 1/3 Brazil** is a series devoted to in-depth examination of the most important Brazilian albums of the twentieth and twenty-first centuries.

Published Titles:

Caetano Veloso's *A Foreign Sound* by Barbara Browning
Tim Maia's *Tim Maia Racional Vols. 1 &2* by Allen Thayer
João Gilberto and Stan Getz's *Getz/Gilberto* by Brian McCann
Gilberto Gil's *Refazenda* by Marc A. Hertzman
Dona Ivone Lara's *Sorriso Negro* by Mila Burns
Milton Nascimento and Lô Borges's *The Corner Club* by Jonathon Grasse
Racionais MCs' *Sobrevivendo no Inferno* by Derek Pardue
Naná Vasconcelos's *Saudades* by Daniel B. Sharp
Chico Buarque's First *Chico Buarque* by Charles A. Perrone

Forthcoming titles:
Jorge Ben Jor's *África Brasil* by Frederick J. Moehn

33 1/3 Europe

Series Editor: Fabian Holt

Spanning a range of artists and genres, **33 1/3 Europe** offers engaging accounts of popular and culturally significant albums of Continental Europe and the North Atlantic from the twentieth and twenty-first centuries.

Published Titles:

Darkthrone's *A Blaze in the Northern Sky* by Ross Hagen
Ivo Papazov's *Balkanology* by Carol Silverman
Heiner Müller and Heiner Goebbels's *Wolokolamsker Chaussee* by Philip V. Bohlman

33 1/3 Oceania

Series Editors: Jon Stratton (senior editor) and Jon Dale (specializing
in books on albums from Aotearoa/New Zealand)Spanning a range
of artists and genres from Australian Indigenous artists to Maori and
Pasifika artists, from Aotearoa/New Zealand noise music to Australian
rock, and including music from Papua and other Pacific islands,
33 1/3 Oceania offers exciting accounts of albums that illustrate the
wide range of music made in the Oceania region.

Kollaps

Melle Jan Kromhout and Jan Nieuwenhuis

Series Editor: Fabian Holt

BLOOMSBURY ACADEMIC
NEW YORK • LONDON • OXFORD • NEW DELHI • SYDNEY

BLOOMSBURY ACADEMIC
Bloomsbury Publishing Inc
1385 Broadway, New York, NY 10018, USA
50 Bedford Square, London, WC1B 3DP, UK
29 Earlsfort Terrace, Dublin 2, Ireland

BLOOMSBURY, BLOOMSBURY ACADEMIC and the Diana logo are
trademarks of Bloomsbury Publishing Plc

First published in the United States of America 2024
Reprinted 2024

Bloomsbury Publishing Inc does not have any control over, or
responsibility for, any third-party websites referred to or in this book. All
internet addresses given in this book were correct at the time of going
to press. The author and publisher regret any inconvenience caused if
addresses have changed or sites have ceased to exist, but can accept no
responsibility for any such changes.

Whilst every effort has been made to locate copyright holders the
publishers would be grateful to hear from any person(s) not here
acknowledged.

A catalog record for this book is available from the Library of Congress.

ISBN: HB: 978-1-5013-8749-4
PB: 978-1-5013-8750-0
ePDF: 978-1-5013-8752-4
eBook: 978-1-5013-8751-7

Typeset by Deanta Global Publishing Services, Chennai, India
Printed and bound in Great Britain

Series: 33 1/3 Europe

To find out more about our authors and books visit www.bloomsbury.com
and sign up for our newsletters.

Contents

the band returned throughout their career, this is expressed with the key phrase 'desire is the only energy'. As the driving force behind their tumultuous, unruly music, it emphasizes Einstürzende Neubauten's unwavering desire to break free.

Together, these eight chapters create a pluriform analysis of *Kollaps*, highlighting the many angles from which the record can be heard and understood. They do not tell a linear story, but jump from one side of the record to the next, to sometimes discuss a song in detail and then focus intensely on a string of tracks, a relevant concept or a particular story. As such, the book goes back and forth, connecting dots while opening up towards the numerous stories and ideas the album contains.

Until the last moment, the record kept changing our own perspectives as well. Even more than we expected when we began writing this book, *Kollaps* continued to talk back to us. We wish for it to resonate in unexpected ways with you too.

Prologue
Stahlmusik

1 April 1980, West-Berlin, Federal Republic of Germany: First concert of Einstürzende Neubauten at the Moon Diskothek in Berlin-Wilmersdorf. Line-up: Blixa Bargeld, N.U. Unruh, Beate Bartel and Gudrun Gut.[1]

April 1980–July 1981: Einstürzende Neubauten played roughly fifteen concerts with changing line-ups. Mostly in West-Berlin.

May 1980: First concert recording released as *Live in Kunstkopfstereo*. Eisengrau. Cassette. 20 copies.[2]

May 1980: Blixa Bargeld and N.U. Unruh at Music Lab Studio in Berlin-Kreuzberg, recording *Fuer den Untergang*. Released September 1980. Monogam. 7" vinyl single.

1 June 1980: Blixa Bargeld and N.U. Unruh in a crawl space in the pillar of a highway underpass in Berlin-Friedenau, recording *Stahlmusik*. Released October 1980. Eisengrau. Cassette. 300 copies.

June 1980: Second concert recording released as *Chaos →Sehnsucht/Energie*. Eisengrau. Cassette. 20 copies.

September 1980: Blixa Bargeld and N.U. Unruh join Alexander Hacke (using the pseudonym Die Sentimentale Jugend) at Music Lab Studio and Cassettencombinat Studio in Berlin-Schöneberg, recording songs for the *Monogam Sampler*. Released February 1981. Monogram. Vinyl LP.

27 December 1980: Blixa Bargeld, N.U. Unruh and Alexander Hacke play at Markthalle, Hamburg. First concert outside of Berlin. Introduction to F.M. Einheit.

April 1981: Blixa Bargeld, N.U. Unruh and Alexander Hacke at Cassettencombinat Studio, recording 'Bakterien für eure Seele'. Released on the compilation album *Lieber Zuviel als Zuwenig (ZickZack Sommerhits 81)*. June 1981. Zickzack. Vinyl LP.

April/May 1981: Blixa Bargeld, N.U. Unruh and F.M. Einheit at Hafenklang Studio, Hamburg, recording *Kalte Sterne*. Released July 1981. Zickzack. 2 x 7" vinyl single.

June 1981: Blixa Bargeld, N.U. Unruh and F.M. Einheit (occasionally joined by Marc Chung) at Hafenklang Studio, Hamburg, recording *Kollaps*. 'Self-recorded/mixed/cut + overdubbed between June-August 81/drums abolished/only metal'.[3]

4 September 1981: Die große Untergangs-Show – Festival Genialer Dilletanten at Berlin Tempodrom, organized by Blixa Bargeld and Wolfgang Müller. Einstürzende Neubauten perform alongside other acts from the Berliner underground.

5 October 1981: *Kollaps* released by Zickzack, an independent record label from Hamburg, founded by music journalist Alfred Hilsberg. Vinyl LP.

1.	Tanz Debil	**8.**	Kollaps
2.	Steh auf Berlin	**9.**	Sehnsucht
3.	Negativ Nein	**10.**	Vorm Krieg
4.	U-Haft Muzak	**11.**	Hirnsäge
5.	Draussen ist Feindlich	**12.**	Abstieg & Zerfall
6.	Schmerzen Hören	**13.**	Helga
7.	Jet'm		

'Our music doesn't come from machines.'[4]

'Love songs are possible.'[5]

Steh auf Berlin
West-Berlin, 1980

The story of Einstürzende Neubauten begins with a very particular city: West-Berlin. More than any other European city, it was affected by the capricious trajectory of twentieth-century history, and it effectively ceased to exist as such with the fall of the Iron Curtain in 1989. A city is like a living organism, its singular character shaped by the lives and actions of the inhabitants, who, in return, are shaped by the city they inhabit. Through this continuous back and forth, Einstürzende Neubauten and West-Berlin are inextricably linked.

At least until the early nineteenth century, walls and moats separated most European cities from the surrounding countryside and city dwellers from countrymen. The borders of modern cities, however, are more diffuse. Having grown excessively since the start of the Industrial Revolution, they sprawl outward. Without clear borders, it can be hard to determine where cities end and countryside begins. In West-Berlin, in the second half of the twentieth century, however, the unambiguous demarcation came back with a vengeance as a wall once again enclosed the city on all sides.

For twenty-eight years, from 1961 to 1989, Berlin was not one but two cities: East and West. The division began when the victorious Allies divided occupied Germany in 1945. The Western part of the country was cut into three zones administered by the United States, Britain and France and the Eastern part comprised a fourth zone, governed by the Soviet Union. Although Berlin was situated in this Russian zone, the former capital of the German Reich received a similar treatment: the Western Allies governed three zones in the Western half of the city, and East Berlin came under Soviet rule. When, in 1949, two separate states were established, the western Federal Republic of Germany (FRG) and the eastern German Democratic Republic (GDR), the division of Germany and Berlin became permanent. On the map, West-Berlin became a capitalist island in communist East Germany.

The Cold War intensified throughout the 1950s, but Berliners could initially still travel from one half of their city to the other, going to work or visiting family and friends, thereby effectively crossing the border between the two German states. However, as tensions between the world powers of the Eastern and Western blocs further rose and the economic situation of the FRG and the GDR drifted apart, more and more East German citizens used the open border in Berlin as a gateway to West Germany and Western Europe. So, by the early 1960s, the East German authorities took drastic measures: on 13 August 1961, they began the construction of a wall around all of West-Berlin. From this day onward, for its roughly two million inhabitants, designated 'transit routes' controlled by the East German authorities, were the only direct connections to travel to and from the rest of the world.

By 1980, the wall had become a terrifying structure. It actually consisted of two walls, the largest 3.6 metres high, separated by 100-metre-wide strip of no man's land filled with landmines and barbed wire. The entire border was guarded by watchtowers manned by guards with the explicit order to shoot anyone who tried to cross from east to west. Closed off from the outside world, the West-Berlin island was economically dependent on its West German mainland. Yet, it did not have an official seat in parliament and remained under the direct military supervision of the Allies. Shaped by the forces of history and unable to control its own destiny, it had become a scarred and derelict half-city.

For people born from the mid-1950s onward, this peculiar situation was just how things were. For young Berlin native Christian Emmerich, born in 1959 and better known to the world as Blixa Bargeld, for instance, 'Berlin . . . represented absolute zero, the starting point where everything is normal'.[1] Yes, the surroundings were bleak, the geopolitical situation was tense and the economy remained unstable, but exactly because of this, housing was extremely cheap and the inhabitants of West-Berlin were exempted from military service. These conditions attracted people from all over Germany and the rest of Europe. They made the West-Berlin squat scene one of the biggest and most fertile in the world and turned the city into a perfect breeding ground for artists, musicians, outsiders and misfits.

In 1980, twenty-year-old Bargeld lived in a residential building with its 'front house bombed out, the back house bombed out, and only the side wing standing', without proper sanitation or warm water, but with 'an enormous garden'.[2] It perfectly illustrates the paradoxical state the city was in: despite the economic hardship and the confinement in an enclave, the historically unique situation produced possibilities that were hard to come by, in Germany or anywhere else in the West. It offered, as Bargeld put it, a unique 'window of opportunity' for the emergence of ideas, sounds and expressions that challenged the dominant middle-class conservatism of the West German and Western European cultural and political mainstream.[3]

In West-Berlin, the past could not be ignored. The city wore its history on its surface, because the devastating results of the Second World War, which had reduced most German cities to rubble, were still omnipresent. Unlike cities like Hamburg or München, where reconstruction had already been well underway in the 1950s and 1960s, in Berlin, large-scale restoration and renovation did not start until the mid-1980s. So, in 1980, the city was still full of what Bargeld called 'scarred terrain'.[4] In almost every street, there were empty plots where apartment blocks once stood. Especially in neighbourhoods directly adjacent to the wall, such as Kreuzberg and Neukölln, old buildings that survived were often poorly maintained. In some areas, like the once traffic-heavy Potsdamer Platz, the whole cityscape lay open: formerly populous neighbourhoods were reduced to unused wasteland.

The very fabric of the city seemed to look backwards, with 'its face turned toward the past'. This is how, at the outset of the Second World War, philosopher Walter Benjamin, born in Berlin in 1892, described what he called the 'angel of history'.[5] Looking towards the past, it sees history as 'one single catastrophe, which keeps piling wreckage upon wreckage and hurls it at his feet'. While the present keeps slipping into the past, the angel of history witnesses the ongoing destruction, but because the storm of progress 'has got caught in his wings' and 'drives him irresistibly into the future', he is unable to save all that is lost. Benjamin's depiction of history, always progressing while leaving the past in ruins, vividly captures the circumstances under which Einstürzende Neubauten emerged: surrounded by the ruins and remains of the past but driven towards the future. They realized, however, that the wreckage was full of potential. With the right mindset, a wasteland becomes a building plot.

This interplay between past, present and future applies not only to physical space (cities, streets, buildings and monuments) but to ideological space as well. Germany's rich cultural, philosophical and musical tradition had been irrevocably tainted by Nazi propaganda and the horrors of the Holocaust.[6] The literal wasteland of its ruined cities thus also symbolized a cultural wasteland. The 'old' was not just physically but also ideologically ruined. As such, younger generations of artists were unable to unproblematically use, reference or access their own countries' cultural history. Many post-war German artists therefore looked for ways to simultaneously confront the past and forge a fresh start. During the twelve years of Nazi dictatorship between 1933 and 1945, culminating in genocide and all-destructive war, the ending of almost everything already occurred. There was no going back, but those willing to venture into uncharted territory found ideal circumstances for exploring new terrain. For Einstürzende Neubauten and their fellow artists, the only way was through. Just as the scarred terrain of West-Berlin offered opportunities to make good use of the physical debris, they aimed for 'the breaking down of thought monuments'.[7] By repurposing the past, they lit the spark of the future.

However, the West-Berliner freedom-in-containment and its joyful celebration of past destruction came with a price, because the future was equally problematic. In isolated West-Berlin, the threat of the Cold War was never far away, and the fear of nuclear annihilation perhaps more palpable than anywhere else. So, notwithstanding the destruction that already took place, an even more definite ending loomed on the horizon. The old buildings were ruined, but the new buildings (*Neubauten*) might collapse (*einstürzen*) just as well. For young people in the Berliner underground, this awareness of impending doom was part of their daily experience. 'People would make jokes about it', remembers Alexander Hacke, who turned fifteen in 1980; 'my Armageddon champagne is waiting in the fridge already'.[8] Yet, for some, exactly this nihilistic outset provided the primary drive for artistic expression. Although Hacke 'didn't really seriously believe that [he] would actually live to see eighteen', if tomorrow might indeed not come, what else is there to do than seize the day?[9]

Bargeld, for one, looked forward to the collapse, and on Einstürzende Neubauten's debut 7" single *Fuer den Untergang* (For the Downfall), released in September 1980, he happily welcomed it with song and dance.[10] A few months earlier, on 1 June, Bargeld and Andrew Chudy (born 1957), alias N.U. Unruh, climbed in a dark and cramped space, five metres wide, fifty metres long and less than one and a half metres high. It looked 'like a mineshaft. A half-hour away from the last bus-stop, it lies directly under a heavily travelled thoroughfare in the southwest part of the city, situated beneath the northeast pillar of a highway underpass.[11] Armed with an untuned guitar, a drum kit and a transistor radio used as amplifier, Bargeld and Unruh recorded the forty-minute *Stahlmusik* (Steel Music) cassette, making good use of the metal walls and massive reverberations of the crawl space.[12]

At the time, the two men already recorded *Fuer den Untergang*'s A-side in a regular music studio in May, but the single's B-side contained the 'Stahlversion' (Steel Version) of the song, recorded during the *Stahlmusik* session in June. This version might be the perfect example of Einstürzende Neubauten's earliest incarnation. Backed by deep, low bangs and the clattering of metal sheets, amplified by the crawl space's exceptionally long reverberations, Bargeld somewhat randomly strums his guitar and repeats over and over again: 'Dance, dance, dance the downfall / Energy collapses.'[13] Off-putting and exhilarating in equal measure, the muffled sounding five-and-a-half-minute song encapsulates the duality of West-Berlin at the outset of the 1980s. Whereas the slow, heavy banging signifies the dread and anxiety of life in the gloomy half-city, Bargeld's menacing vocals, interpolated by his off-pitch and awkwardly timed guitar squeaks, add an electrifying sense of excitement and anticipation. The lyrics, finally, express the defining sentiment of the West-Berliner underground at the time: if we are going down, we might as well go dancing.

Trapped in-between a tainted and problematic past and a bleak and hopeless future, Einstürzende Neubauten celebrated the cramped space of the present. The music was an expression of their experiences living in the bombed-out houses of Berlin in 1980 and their strategies to occupy and repurpose these ruins. This goes most literally for the city's apartment blocks, which were squatted and turned into creative spaces, but also applies to the discarded materials that the members of Einstürzende Neubauten collected on the city's scrapyards and turned into makeshift musical instruments. These strategies made the city speak, exorcizing the ghosts of Berlin to furiously celebrate its precarious present. For all its seemingly destructive force, this means Einstürzende Neubauten's art exerts a remarkable life-affirming energy.

Somewhat surprisingly, *Kollaps* itself was not recorded in Berlin at all. It was put to tape over the course of several weeks between June and August 1981 in the Hafenklang Studios in Hamburg. Freshly joined band member F.M. Einheit, born Frank-Martin Strauß (1958), already recorded there with his band Abwärts and arranged for its use. Still, Bargeld and Unruh brought their hometown with them, and *Kollaps* can very much be heard as a sonification of West-Berlin in the early 1980s. This is most explicit on the album's second song, 'Steh auf Berlin' (Stand Up Berlin or Go for Berlin).[14]

It begins with the sound of drilling; thirty seconds filled with the dull noise of maintenance work. As Italian artist and composer Luigi Russolo wrote in his 1913 futurist manifesto *The Art of Noise*, such construction sounds have defined the 'pounding atmosphere of great cities' ever since the beginning of the Industrial Revolution.[15] When the pneumatic drill grinds to a halt, frantic drumming begins – metal bars on metal plates. 'In the squatters' street battles against local authorities', Bargeld recalls, 'people started to build barricades and they drummed for hours on the fences and barricades'.[16] On 'Steh auf Berlin', the barricades become musical instruments, transporting the listeners to the streets of West-Berlin, overhearing the riot. They are in the thick of it, riled up by Bargeld, as his shrill voice suddenly shouts: '*Aufstehen*' – get up! 'Lie down / scorched earth'[17] Bursts of noise interpolate the beat. 'Stand up! Crash! Collapse!' The song is propelled forward by the relentless drumming of Einheit and Unruh, and calling the rioters into action, Bargeld spits out his words: 'Steh auf Berlin!'

An early example of the intricate wordplay that would become a hallmark of Bargeld's lyrics, the German word *Aufstehen* has many meanings. It means to get up, rise up or stand up, but also to stand on something, both literally (to stand on the streets and the barricades), but also metaphorically, to insist: 'I insist on fire / I insist on smoke', he sings. 'I insist on noise / and I insist on stones!'[18] Finally, it can mean to go for, to fancy or even to love something or somebody. 'I love sickness / I love downfall / I am up for the end!'[19] Thus, 'Steh auf Berlin' also means 'love Berlin!' Despite the nihilistic lyrical imagery and rough sound, all these layers of positive and negative meanings and associations add up to reveal a song of defiance. 'Steh auf Berlin' is an appeal to stand up and rise from the ashes. To take the ruins, rubble and debris as inspiring resources and build new instruments, explore different sounds and embrace an absolute love of life.

'In school', Bargeld wrote, 'I was taught that music and architecture are closely connected. Palaces are built like classical symphonies. Now, our music should also be built (like the houses we live in), like demolished houses, like normal houses'[20] True to this vision, *Kollaps* combines the sonification of urban desolation with the excitement of social unrest. It sardonically celebrates decline and downfall as the grim reality of late-capitalist society in the last outpost of the self-proclaimed 'free world', but without self-pity or spiteful accusation. The album is an act of celebration, a refusal to mourn the downfall and instead 'mirror the uglier aspects of the city only to distort them to such an extent they appear beautiful'.[21]

The titular moment of the 'collapse', finally, must therefore be understood as an impetus to wipe the slate clean and make music no one has made before. Music that truly resonates with the scarred streets and derelict houses of West-Berlin and celebrates all the possibilities and promises they hold. The new is always already old. Decay sets in as soon as new buildings are erected. But underneath the rubble, the first signs of unimagined possibilities are waiting for someone brave enough to dig them up and accept the challenge.

Kollaps
Berliner underground

'A hammer', Blixa Bargeld proclaimed, 'is substantially more of a musical instrument than a guitar'.[1] This statement is easily aligned with others, for instance, where he insisted to never tune his guitar or practise his playing. In fact, Bargeld frequently confirmed he could not play the guitar at all, let alone repeat anything he had played before.[2] He was no virtuoso, to say the least. His style was born from a reluctance to master the instrument. Bargeld's statements therefore illustrate what it meant for him to make music: effecting change. 'A hammer', he explained, 'can accomplish something (changes, effects), while a guitar amplifies vibrations and produces tones that wouldn't even leave an imprint on a wall, let alone hammer in a nail'.[3] Driving a nail in a wall with a hammer is no problem. Neither is using it to punch a hole in the wall, though it might require a bit more force.

Bargeld did not entirely disqualify the guitar. He played it for many years and ultimately even mastered his 'inability-to-play'. Still, the comparison between a tool and a musical instrument tells us something about his creative mentality: to prefer a hammer over a guitar means preferring creation over reproduction. Using a hammer to make music requires the invention of playing techniques and results in unexpected sounds. A hammer, in short, demands a different musical attitude that unleashes unknown forces. It is an instrument for building.

Whereas the inability to play an instrument would be disadvantageous to most musicians, in West-Berlin in the early 1980s, it was considered an asset that allowed people without musical training to enter the world of music. Many such musicians populated the scene that came to be known as Geniale Dilletanten (*Brilliant dilletantes* [*sic*]).

The name first appeared on a self-made pin that adorned Bargeld's jacket in the summer of 1981. That same year, on 4 September, one month before the release of *Kollaps*, Bargeld and artist Wolfgang Müller organized a festival called Die große Untergangs-Show – Festival Genialer Dilletanten (The Great Downfall-Show – Brilliant Dilletants' Festival). It brought together a very diverse group of artists who all challenged accepted notions of music and musicianship. Alongside Einstürzende Neubauten, it featured performances by Din A Testbild, Sprung aus den Wolken, Sentimentale Jugend, saxophone player Frieder Butzmann and Müller's band Die Tödliche Doris.

Traditionally, a dilettante is an amateur who loves to make art or play music without making it into a profession. Müller sees the intentional spelling mistake in the name of the West-Berlin scene (adding an 'l' and removing a 't') as a positive error that marks a deviation from this traditional meaning.[4] As such, the name works on at least two levels: firstly, a mistake can be a viable point of departure for creativity. It is something that falls outside of the expected scheme of things and breaks a rule, thus stretching the playing field. The realm of what is thought to be possible suddenly expands. Secondly, adopting a pejorative term as something positive neutralizes its original meaning. The name, thus, plays with the artificial divide between so-called professionals (the virtuoso insiders) and the outside amateurs. Changing dilettante to dilletant creates a platform for the brilliant amateurs to perform their music. It breaks with the cult of the artist as genius.

The Festival Genialer Dilletanten created a possibility for the artists to perform on stage together, but the legend surrounding the festival outgrew the actual event.[5] Bargeld later called it a 'coup de presse', confirming that the moniker Geniale Dilletanten primarily functioned as a keyword for the media.[6] Indeed, as a coherent musical denominator, Geniale Dilletanten lacked an overarching identity. The playful irony of Die Tödliche Doris, for instance, contrasts heavily with the ecstatic din of Einstürzende Neubauten, and except for the sound of the German language, there is a world of difference between Din A Testbild's rhythm-driven synth music and the stripped-bare songs of Sprung aus den Wolken. The bands and artists that performed at the festival and came to be associated with Geniale Dilletanten did not share many musical characteristics and were too diverse to form a coherent artist collective. In fact, their single common desire was to be no part of anything anyway.

Still, although Geniale Dilletanten rebelled against institutionalized music, their approach ultimately did become a category in itself. This is partly due to the publication, a year after the festival, of a book called *Geniale Dilletanten*, edited by Müller and largely written by himself, using several pseudonyms.[7] Very much of interest as a historical document, it is not a manifesto containing the next best truism in art, but Müller's compilation of the ideas shared by this group of musicians and artists (almost like an artwork in and of itself) does certainly express a sense of belonging and shared set of values. What the group lacked in similarities in style, approach and sound, they made up for in terms of collective mentality. The name Geniale Dilletanten is therefore still often used to capture the blooming West-Berlin artist scene of the early 1980s.[8] Because it became a label for the cultural expression of a particular group of people at a particular point in time.

This is best reflected through their choice of language. Most German popular music from the preceding eras had been influenced by British and American music and was sung in English. One notable exception is the rock band Ton Steine Scherben.[9] Based in West-Berlin, starting with their debut record in 1971, they were among the first acts to use German in their name, song titles and lyrics. Their example was followed by German punk bands like Hans-A-Plast, Abwärts and Mittagspause and the reappropriation of their own language also echoed among the Geniale Dilletanten. After everything associated with Germanness had been contaminated by the Second World War, here was a chance to begin anew. 'We hate our culture and our language', Bargeld said, 'all our philosophy and music was appropriated by the Nazis: Durer [sic], Bach, Friedrich N-Punkt! We cannot redeem that tradition. We can only re-invent'.[10] The do-it-yourself attitude and repurposing of the German language by the punk movement served as an act of self-empowerment.

Geniale Dilletanten were members of a younger generation that tried to shape their own history.

Musically, however, 'punk was only Rock'n'Roll in fast, so nothing special'.[11] Although its aggressive sound paved the way for louder noises, punk did not really catch on with the West-Berliner underground. They were far more interested in the abstract and free-spirited music of the No-New-York scene with bands and artists like Mars, DNA and Teenage Jesus and the Jerks. Bargeld also listened to a lot of reggae.[12] 'The musical reservoir was wide', he said, 'it was not just Sex Pistols. They bored me from the start'.[13] N.U. Unruh liked Throbbing Gristle and Glenn Branca. More than just personal taste, these wide-ranging preferences illustrate the musical direction that Einstürzende Neubauten and the Dilletanten were taking. Punk was merely a catalyst for developing a completely different music.

Even beyond music, techniques from the visual arts provided a fertile stimulus; especially Dada. In the first decades of the twentieth century, Dada artists got rid of rules altogether. 'Dada is not an axiom', Richard Huelsenbeck wrote in his introduction to the 1920 *Dada Almanac*. 'Dada is a state of mind independent of all schools and theories, one that addresses individuality itself without doing violence to it. One cannot reduce Dada to principles'.[14] Dada embraced the complexities of modern life and celebrated the abundance of free-floating ideas. It did not respect the traditional techniques of painting, writing, composing, performing and other forms of art. Understood as sacrilege, Dada does just that: kicking down sacred cows.[15]

Especially everything that was not considered art by the established art world attracted the attention of Dada artists.

Marcel Duchamp famously submitted his sculpture *Fountain* to the 1917 exhibition of the Society of Independent Artists. It was a urinal. Kurt Schwitters used public transport tickets, newspaper clippings and candy wrappers in his paintings. This use of found objects drastically changed the notion of what art can be and what an artist should be capable of. Moreover, Dada radically departed from art's etymological root. The Latin *ars* denotes skill or craft, but from a Dada point of view, the 'idea' prevails over technique. An artist no longer has to be a trained craftsman. Duchamp changed nothing about his piece of sanitary hardware. He bought it and moved it to an exhibition space. By doing so, he made room; revealing a space in art where meaning can transform.

For Dada, art can be anything, and anything can be art. When candy wrappers are unwrapped and bus tickets are validated, they lose their value. Nothing more than pieces of paper remains. But when Schwitters substituted paint for old paper, he found something beautiful and positive in the debris of everyday life. The same goes for the West-Berliner Dilletants. The remains of everyday life, for instance, echo through Din A Testbild's first release, a 7" single called *Abfall Garbage/Glas Konkav* (1979).[16] It came in a plastic bag filled with candy wrappers, jigsaw puzzle pieces, shreds of wallpaper and other material. Similarly, Einstürzende Neubauten used tape-loops, found sounds and construction tools to make their music. If a bus ticket can be part of a painting, a jackhammer might as well be a musical instrument. The objects are deliberately transplanted from their original context into another one. The shattering glass and construction tools on 'Steh auf Berlin' become an inherent part of the music, equal to Bargeld's voice and untuned guitar.

'Dada cannot be justified by any system that approaches people with "Thou shalt"', wrote Huelsenbeck. 'Dada rests within itself and acts of its own accord, just as the sun acts when it rises in the sky or when a tree grows.'[17] For Einstürzende Neubauten, and the other Dilletants as well, music was similarly connected to life. Not as an artistic representation or illusory painting, but as a force of nature – an act of creation. Einstürzende Neubauten were not interested in entertainment, which only serves to distract from impending doom. They wanted to create music that could make sense of the complexity of their world, because making music meant effecting change. They only needed the right attitude and the right instruments to do so.

Kollaps is born from this mentality: music shapes life. The record, says Bargeld, was '[a] sweeping blow for freedom, to break away from the feeling that one has to make something that anybody likes. But amazingly', he continues, 'in spite of everything it did please some people.'[18] In fact, the record touched listeners exactly because it did not pretend to be something it was not. Contrary to most mainstream popular music, it did not feed its audience idealistic music to conceal the struggles and worries of everyday life. Instead, Einstürzende Neubauten grounded their music in the experience of a particular place at a particular time. They did not follow the tracks of existing musical practices, but all the bits and pieces they could use, they made their own, filtered through the experiences of life in West-Berlin.

A widely shared feeling among the West-Berlin artists was that Germany, as an exponent of Western culture, had failed and was irrevocably broken. As a result, it was even gullible to tune a guitar, because by doing this, one blindly follows an age-old tuning system that prescribes how to make music. To deliberately refrain from tuning meant taking a stance against tradition and acknowledging that Western tonality is an invention like any other. Usable, at times, but attached to a cultural history and ideology that had become obsolete. Traditional music did not resonate with their world view because it carried too much historical weight. Einstürzende Neubauten and their peers therefore chipped away at the core of Western music, discarding and desecrating its harmonies, tonalities and the supposed professionalism and virtuosity of conventional instruments.

This disregard for Western tonality and virtuosity emancipated musical creation and made it available to more people. Combined with easier access to electronic instruments like drum machines and synthesizers and the production of self-made instruments from scrap metal, it inspired a cultural practice more akin to, in Bargeld's words, 'modern folk' than to art music: 'folk which is as close to us as the folk music 2000 years ago was to the people at that time. This is the real psycho-beat, the rhythm which is in us. Because it is the rhythm which is around us'.[19] The shift to German as the dominant language further enhanced this sense of collective identity.

For the Geniale Dilletanten, how and what kind of music one made was no longer restricted by theories, dogmas or other rules, but this communal rejection of traditional musical values did express a deeply rooted wish to belong. Although they were not in a position to change the world powers that ruled West-Berlin, these artists chose to reorganize their lives and create their own communal and genuinely human music. The music of Einstürzende Neubauten, as the most outspoken exponent of this mindset, was therefore intimately connected to the incongruity and uncertainty of living in West-Berlin in the early 1980s. The music suited the city and its inhabitants.

Ultimately, Geniale Dilletanten were first and foremost, an invitation to join the carnival. Beyond its celebration of destruction, downfall and decay, *Kollaps* is a natural counterpart to life itself. As a result, the record is brimming with possibilities. The songs on the album are as stylistically different from each other as the bands that populated West-Berlin in the early 1980s. The record even includes a genuine chanson and fragments of jazz. And yet, this diversity makes perfect sense because it attempts to grapple with the complexities of life by celebrating its abundance. Each song has its own internal coherence; each sound takes on new meanings, but the album as a whole is about transforming what already exists. The driving force behind the record is a restless ingenuity. With a total disregard for existing structures and rules, Bargeld, Einheit and Unruh revelled in their unrefined virtuosity of ideas.[20]

Tanz Debil
Transgressing the stage

In the early days, Einstürzende Neubauten were not about skill, musical competence, subtle song writing or lyrical nuance. They were all attitude, sense of purpose and provocative gesture. To be a performer, Blixa Bargeld explained, you only have to 'stand on a chair and start screaming at the wrong moment'.[1] In other words, just climb on stage and bang and scream like your life depends on it. Seduce the audience and rile them up with sheer volume and manic intensity. For the downfall! Listen with pain! Debility dance!

At centre stage stood Bargeld, his long, thin figure dressed in a black rubber coat. Pale as a ghost, his hair haphazardly cut with a razor blade, causing bald patches on his skull, he looked 'like Death in rubber boots'.[2] A 'thoroughly fucked guitar' was casually strapped around his shoulder, but never used in a conventional way: no strumming or delicate fingerpicking, virtuosic solos or shredding power chords.[3] The untuned strings were only hit and strangled at the wrong moment, which to him, of course, was exactly right. Bargeld shouted his lyrics into the microphone, furiously spitting words towards the audience. His screams were not yet the infamously prolonged, whistle-register wails he would develop later, but profoundly chilling nonetheless.

The frontman was flanked by two percussionists. Firstly, N.U. Unruh – a member of the band from its inception, alongside Bargeld. He had been interested in sound and noise from an early age and was especially fascinated by reverberance: the sounds produced when objects begin to vibrate.[4] Before returning to his native Berlin, Unruh briefly trained as a piano tuner in Amsterdam. A piano, after all, is nothing but eighty-eight tiny hammers banging on strings housed in a reverberating box of wood and metal. Not long after the foundation of the band, Unruh sold his drum kit. Allegedly out of financial necessity, but building a replacement kit from scrapyard material also conveniently matched his appetite for sound exploration and instrument building.

Secondly, the often-bare-chested F.M. Einheit smashed metal on metal and handled power tools alongside Unruh. He already played drums in various punk bands in Hamburg before joining Einstürzende Neubauten in the spring of 1981. Einheit's sharply focused, steady and ferocious drum skills added extra groove and energy to the band's music, and his flair for stage theatrics enhanced the drama of their performances.

This trio – Bargeld, Unruh, Einheit – recorded *Kollaps*, but the other two members of the five-person line-up that existed until the mid-1990s were already around as well. Alexander Hacke – also known at the time as Alexander von Borsig – was only fourteen years old in 1980 but very active in various bands and as a solo artist. He joined Einstürzende Neubauten on stage on multiple occasions, playing guitar, drums or bass. Not long after the release of *Kollaps*, the other band members temporarily sent him away, but Hacke still frequently operated the mixing console in rather unconventional ways. He rejoined as a full-time band member in 1983.[5] Bassist Marc Chung, finally, played together with Einheit in Hamburg and was asked to contribute 'some bass frequencies' on *Kollaps*'s title track.[6] He joined the band shortly before the record's release.

At Einstürzende Neubauten's debut performance on 1 April 1980 at the Moon Diskothek in Berlin-Wilmersdorf, however, only the core duo of Bargeld on vocals and guitar and Unruh on (still conventional) drum kit was present. They were joined by Beate Bartel on bass and Gudrun Gut on synthesizer. A recording of this show (Einstürzende Neubauten's first release of any kind) appeared a month later on a cassette called *Live in Kunstkopfstereo* (Live in Dummy Head Stereo), limited to twenty copies. Although the band further developed its singular style through their increasingly ferocious live performances over the course of the following year, a close listen to this recording from their first concert confirms that the most fundamental aspects of their music were almost fully formed from the beginning.

There is no trace yet of the scrap-metal-drumming and power-tool-wielding intensity that was to come, but the signature rhythmic groundwork that defines *Kollaps* can already be heard in the interplay between Bargeld's guitar, Unruh's drumming and Bartel's throbbing bass. The foundation of each of the four tracks is laid by a simple, repetitive drum rhythm and continuously struck dissonant guitar chords. Gut's synthesizer serves as a noise maker, providing the kind of disruptive interpolations that would later be produced by jackhammers, feedback noise and pneumatic drills. Instantly recognizable, finally, are Bargeld's deadpan vocals: 'Greed! Greed! Greed! Greed!' he shouts over and over again on the eponymously titled 'Gier' – lyrics that would later appear on *Kollaps*'s opening song, 'Tanz Debil' (Debility Dance). Throughout the set, Bargeld's voice provides a focal point that keeps the tumultuous music from falling apart.

These earliest songs are noisy, under-rehearsed and decisively amateurish, but listening beyond the tape hiss and poor recording quality to the ferocity of the band's delivery and the conviction in Bargeld's voice, it is clear they meant business. Even at this first concert, the two guiding principles of Einstürzende Neubauten's music are firmly in place: repetition and contingency. Principally, in its most elementary form, almost all music can be defined by the sounding interplay between repeating elements (whether rhythmic, melodic, harmonic or timbral) and the introduction and further development of more contingent or incidental elements. Yet, in the early work of Einstürzende Neubauten, this interplay is the main concern. Stripped of all other musical elements, such as harmonic structuring, melodic development, timbral colouration and compositional growth, it is all that remains. The interplay between repetition and contingency is what this music is all about.

During the band's early performances, simple repetitive figures drew rough outlines of songs: a bass line, a guitar squeak, a drum beat or, in many cases, Bargeld's voice. They grounded the pieces and often carried over from one show to the next. As such, given the fundamentally improvisational nature of the music, these elements provided recognizable seeds from which the pieces could further evolve. Because noise and disorder frequently threatened to overtake the senses, these repetitive pulses, rhythms or vocal lines functioned as lifelines for the audience to hold on to. Despite Bargeld's assertion that he 'could never repeat what [he] once played', then, it would be a mistake to think that everything on stage happened in the spur of the moment.[7] In fact, over the course of consecutive performances and rehearsals, improvisation turned into composition, and more definable songs took shape. Certain sounds, rhythms, structures and lyrics that appear on *Kollaps* can already be heard on these recordings of the band's earliest live shows.

Bargeld's ambition for the band's work, to be 'far enough away from music that nobody can tell you anymore what the rules are for what we are doing', does therefore not actually ring true.[8] On the contrary, Einstürzende Neubauten's early work actually highlights some of music's most elementary principles. Grounded by simple repetitive elements that define the pieces from one iteration to the next, their songs further developed on the spot by adding unexpected, incidental and more contingent sounds and noises each time around. As a result, song templates carried over from one show to the next, but no performance was ever the same. If only because Bargeld never tuned his guitar, which meant that the sound of each show depended on the accidental tuning of his strings. Precisely this tensive back and forth between grounding repetition and random, incidental, unexpected and contingent elements made each performance thrilling, captivating and exciting.

After playing a handful of shows, Bartel and Gut went their separate way, reducing Einstürzende Neubauten to its atomic nucleus, with Bargeld and Unruh as proton and neutron.[9] The chemistry between the two founding members is evident on *Stahlmusik*, a forty-minute improvisation which they recorded in the crawl space of a highway underpass on 1 June 1980. Although Unruh still used his regular drum kit, the exceptionally reverberatory space became an instrument in itself. Its floor and walls were used as percussive instruments, and Bargeld's jarring guitar chords and shouting vocals were massively amplified by the room's acoustics. The lo-fi cassette recording of this performance captures Einstürzende Neubauten in its most rudimentary form: an improvised play of heavy percussion, repetitive vocals and shrill guitar noise produced at one specific moment with these specific instruments in this very specific room.

If Bargeld and Unruh, whose artistic collaboration predated the foundation of the band, formed Einstürzende Neubauten's atomic nucleus, the arrival of Einheit provided the electric charge. He met the band at their seventh or eighth concert; their first show outside of Berlin and the first using a homemade scrap-metal drum kit. Hacke accompanied Bargeld and Unruh on the drums. The crowd in Hamburg's Markthalle on 27 December 1980, primarily showed up for a riot, leaving the band members initially unsure whether to play at all. Luckily, after local fan favourite Abwärts went offstage, most people left the venue, and the Berliner's gave a particularly intense performance.[10] This heavily impressed Abwärts drummer Einheit, setting the group on course towards *Kollaps*.

The tension between the three men set everything in motion. And precisely such 'tension [*Spannung*]', Bargeld explained, 'defines the quality of the music'.[11] In physics, *Spannung*, tension or voltage, is the measure of difference in electric potential between two points in a circuit. Following this logic, 'Einstürzende Neubauten' itself can be represented as an electric circuit, and their music can be described in terms of energy flow, electric charge, tension, resistance and feedback. Alternatively, using another physics metaphor, the tension that propels the music forward as the performance gets more and more heated, can be expressed in terms of the second law of thermodynamics, which describes the interplay between entropy (disorder, randomness or chaos) and negentropy (order or repetition). In other words, working against the structuring principle of repetition, which keeps music orderly and well-defined, the introduction of contingent and incidental elements is a reminder that, following the second law of thermodynamics, the steady growth of entropy (disorder, chaos or noise) is inevitable, and order is, at best, temporary.

These metaphors of energy transfer and heat flow are actually part of the band's own discourse. On the brooding 'Sehnsucht' (Desire), the only song on *Kollaps* that already appears on *Stahlmusik*, Bargeld sings: 'Desire / comes out of chaos / desire / is the only energy.'[12] In the record's booklet, these sentences take the form of a pseudo-logical equation: 'Chaos ⇒ Sehnsucht / Energie'.[13] Expressing the relationship between three fundamental forces in the band's work, it might be read like this: the fundamental and inevitable state of *chaos* (randomness, disorder or entropy) equals the driving artistic force of *desire*, divided by the *energy* released by the act of musical performance. To be fair, the point is probably not to make sense of this in such a quasi-literal sense. Rather, the equation stands as an intuitive, metaphorical mission statement underpinning the band's artistic programme. The tension produced by the interplay between chaos, order, repetition, entropy, energy and desire, it says, is what their work is about.

In the band's early live performances, this interplay came most astutely to the fore through the frequent physical transgressions of the band members that sometimes came at the expense of their own bodies. As they were wielding power tools and steel bars, cuts and bruises came with the territory. However, rather than nihilistic violence or mindless aggression, Bargeld explained, this willingness to undergo physical harm was about 'crossing boundaries'.[14] Driven by the desire to reach out and *touch* the audience by all means possible, their self-evasive transgressions can be seen as an attempt to reach levels of intensity that could establish a kind of shared physicality and thereby break down the distance between performer and audience.

These acts of physical transgression at the expense of the band member's own bodies are tokens of vulnerability that express a wish to open up towards the other. As Bargeld describes on 'Schmerzen Hören' (Listen with Pain), the 'ears are wounds'. This music should not only be heard; it has to be felt. As sound moves through the air from one place to the other, from body to body, on the side of the listener, it penetrates the eardrums and makes its way to the brain, creating physical sensations that establish affective relationships. At the same time, on the side of the performers, the effort that goes into producing these sounds is marked on the body in the form of physical scars. Bargeld still remembers the 'corresponding concerts of the five or six scars on my body. The scar above my eyebrow is from the microphone stand in Pula in Yugoslavia. . . . I got the scar on my left hand at a concert in Münster in 1980. . . . These accidents happened out of a certain liveliness and also out of passion'.[15] Thus, just like sound recordings store physical sound waves on material surfaces, scars are physical records of specific performances. They are permanent reminders of transgressive moments when order gave in to chaos.

Einstürzende Neubauten thereby fully embraced the singularity of performative acts. Fully aware that a performance only happens once and cannot be repeated as such, they ferociously approached each show like it was their last. The band members, Hacke recalled, wanted to 'catapult [them] selves into a state . . . where we could leave our own lives and just be inside the music'.[16] With their furious energy, they tried to erase the past, ignore the future and just be here, together, now.[17] Music can achieve this because, as musicologists Daniel Chua and Alexander Rehding write, it 'removes time and space from their normal order, lifting them out of the ordinary and intensifying their qualities'.[18] This ability to play with time is an essential feature of all music, but different types of music relate to and change our sense of time and space in different ways.

In the case of Einstürzende Neubauten, the idea that music is a way of playing with time and space and removing them from their normal order is already contained in the band's name. 'The endpoint of progress', Bargeld explained in 1981, 'is when things no longer grow old but are destroyed again the moment they arise'.[19] Einstürzende Neubauten therefore means that even things that are brand new can collapse at any moment. Only the 'now' is permanent, but permanently changing. In their early days, the bands' performances fully embraced and even celebrated this fundamental impermanence: as soon as music comes into its own, it disappears again. The fruit of the labour, however, is a strong sense of community between the band and its audience, forged by a deep longing to connect.

Schmerzen Hören
Sounding bodies

From the cover of *Kollaps*, a single eye pries back at us. It stares into the distance, motionless, but radiating outwards. The dot that forms the eye is encircled: a big, round head balancing on a slim neck. Underneath, there is a body with two arms and a pair of legs, one shorter than the other. The figure is static, but its disproportionate limbs suggest movement. It dances. It is a mythological icon. An archetypal figure, representing more than one can grasp at first sight. It asks to be filled with meaning, but constantly eludes definition. It is an undefined, manifold body, though very clear in its appearance. Perhaps it represents music itself.

There are different views about Einstürzende Neubauten's logo. Some see it as a cyclops – the one-eyed giants from Greek mythology. Others think it is a double representation of humanity and the sun. F.M. Einheit called it 'a mythological sign, a sorcerer or something like that'.[1] Sometimes, it is even compared to a cross. Alexander Hacke sees the humanoid figure as representing different levels of the world: 'the legs represent the earth, the head, the sky and the point in the centre would represent the sun'.[2] Blixa Bargeld alleged he found the symbol in a book of Mexican cave paintings – a Toltec petroglyph, preceding the Mayan era. For him, the humanoid figure on the cover of *Kollaps* indeed represents the sun. In a diary page from 1983, he elaborates:

The head as sun/eye
human body
as acting
sun + celestial bodies

Acting human
The head encloses the sun,
Is celestial body
Is heaven

This is heaven
Clearly as a human
Is celestial body
The sun is eye
Is the acting sun
That-moves
Man is heaven

The acting sun
Is heaven on earth[3]

The dotted circle, without the body, already appears on the cover of *Kalte Sterne* (Cold Stars), the double 7" single that preceded *Kollaps* by three months. There, it is accompanied by nine rays that extend outwards, suggesting a sun or a star. Indeed, the astronomical symbol for the sun is a circle with a dot in the middle. Einstürzende Neubauten's logo represents an energetic body, capable of feeding life and destroying it through radiation, like the star that fuels our solar system. It is a force comparable to the affective destruction of Einstürzende Neubauten's live performances. The image thereby illustrates the central role of different kinds of bodies in Einstürzende Neubauten's work: the bodies of the band members, the body expressed through Bargeld's singing voice and, finally, the body of music itself.

At Die Große Untergangs-Show – Festival Genialer Dilletanten, on 4 September 1981, Einstürzende Neubauten performed the song 'Kollaps' (Collapse). In the video of the event, Bargeld is seen dressed in his trademark black rubber clothes.[4] He stands in front of two microphones, shouting, 'Kollaps!' His eyes pry in the distance, the left one heavily encircled with black mascara. His iris and pupil form a dot in the white of his eye. He hardly moves, only shifts his weight and strums his guitar from time to time. Gesturing with his right arm and clenching his fist, he emits an immovable force.

This is not just a body performing. It is a body performed – a part in Bargeld's larger project to extract all potential from himself. 'I want to squeeze my body like a lemon', he said, 'and everything that comes out of it must be good because I'm working on the product that is Blixa Bargeld. . . . It is a matter of using your whole person as a test object, putting your whole life forward as an experimental case.'[5] As a result, his identity was in constant flux. Changing one's name, for instance, was a strategy of appropriating yourself: 'it was just in the air that everyone changed their names', Gudrun Gut remembers. 'You invented yourself, you were master of your future, present and past.'[6] Bargeld took his last name from Dada artist Johannes

Theodor Baargeld and his first from a felt-tip pen named Blixa Color 70. The combination of the two created a persona that was hard to pin down: 'my name tended to sound a bit androgynous, because in German, a name that ends with "a" can only be female.'[7] 'Blixa Bargeld' cannot be easily defined or categorized.

Hence, like his music, Bargeld's invented self was not bound by predefined ideas of what a person or a body should be. He represented something undefinable: '[a] transcendent quality, that made him so far outside our puny ideas of earth-gender, that categories of man, woman, human, alien, just seemed inapplicable. . . . He never tried to look like a woman; he always seemed to be trying to look like something beyond gender.'[8] From the very beginning, Bargeld constructed a persona that could be constantly recreated, turning his body into an empty vessel to be filled as he pleased.

In the same vein, to achieve what Einstürzende Neubauten were striving for in music, the other band members also changed themselves and the way they behaved, pushing their own bodies beyond their limits to transgress the boundaries of music making. 'Through our physical efforts at concerts, but also in the studio', said Einheit,

> 'we developed a different kind of music; we reached other realms of consciousness. The most wonderful thing is when you can completely lose your consciousness while making music. But those are moments that happen only very rarely. One means to get to this point of losing one's consciousness is to work your way toward it physically, to reach your physical limits.'[9]

To lose consciousness while making music required going beyond ingrained habits and worn-out preferences and developing a different musical attitude. Exhausting their bodies was therefore part of Einstürzende Neubauten's musical playground, a destructive game they played to make room for the unexpected. So, as they sought to unlearn and dismantle all given musical structures, they challenged and expanded not only their own bodies but also the body of music itself.

This approach finds a theoretical pendant in the work of French writer, poet and dramatist Antonin Artaud (1896–1946), who proclaimed that humanity had lost its freedom to act and its connection to life due to the structures and regulations imposed by modern society. 'Man', writes Artaud, 'is sick because he is badly constructed'. He needs to undergo 'an autopsy in order to remake his anatomy'.[10] Similarly, Einstürzende Neubauten considered the body of music to be badly constructed. Within the confines of existing musical structures, they were unable to make the music they envisioned. Music had come to a standstill and lacked vitality. It was too organized and predictable. At the start of the record, Bargeld shouts, 'Pretend you are dead / pretend you are dead! / Greed! / Pretend you are dead / Greed!' Words that could be an indictment against the commercialization of music. Next, he offers a vitalizing alternative: 'Open my veins / just under my skin.'[11] With Artaud in mind, it sounds like an invitation for an autopsy. Not just on human bodies but on music itself.

Einstürzende Neubauten longed for an unconstrained musical practice. Without prescribed contours or definitions, whether human, sociological, cultural, political, ethical, musical or otherwise, they found freedom in a music imbued with vitality and the joy of discovery. Bargeld did not tune his guitar, N.U. Unruh threw out his regular drum set, and beyond the domain of conventional music, they discovered new sounds: shattering glass, running water or roaring power tools. They even played around with something as straightforward and simple as the duration of a song. On *Kollaps*, there are five that are less than one and a half minutes long: 'Draussen ist Feindlich', 'Jet'm', 'Sehnsucht', 'Vorm Krieg' and 'Helga'.

Even on the level of the songs themselves, there are instances in which their internal organization is explicitly dissected. 'U-Haft Muzak' (Custody Muzak), for instance, carries a calm rhythm, similar to a heartbeat.[12] A voice whistles or sings melodic fragments, from a distance, in a separate auditory space. On top of, and in contrast with, these two consistent elements, however, erratic, bright metal, guitar feedback and the sound of electrical tools add an otherworldly din. 'Draussen ist Feindlich' (Outside is Hostile) is rigidly structured, but the introduction of pestering, pitch-shifting vocals towards the end of the song undermines its order. The same goes for the voice shouting 'Schalt den Film ein!' (Turn on the film!) on 'Jet'm', almost as if one should stop listening to music altogether. With this urge to disturb the musical order and pull a song in a different direction, the band reaches for a music that breaks away from the familiar – even from the music they are creating at that very moment.

Following Artaud, then, music for Einstürzende Neubauten is an unorganized body to be filled as one likes. This offers much more possibilities than a music based on rules and restrictions as to how it should be made. It calls for an attitude of constant renewal and versatility that is already expressed by their band name: 'Einstürzende Neubauten', explained Unruh: 'means the existing, the now, has had its time, it's used up, put into question. Something new is invented. . . . It means constant change. "You must destroy to build"'[13] Nothing should be taken for granted. Existing music needs to collapse.

Artaud's concept of autopsy, finally, is also relevant in relation to Bargeld's singular vocal and lyrical treatment. On *Kollaps*, Bargeld dissects language by reassembling words. In the title track, for instance, he vocally fragments the word 'Kollaps' so that with each repetition, it sounds different. He lengthens the word, almost cutting it in two. Adding a string of notes, he sings it in a melismatic form. He expels the word, spits it out, or jolts out 'Kollaps' like he is gasping for air. Each iteration is sung like the previous one is already forgotten. And each time, Bargeld throws his whole body into ushering a transformative cry. Beyond their linguistic meaning, the words thereby gain the kind of material substance that French philosopher Roland Barthes calls 'the grain of the voice', by which he means the singular presence of the physical body in the (singing) voice.[14] This bodily quality adds meaning through the specific sound of the words rather than their linguistic content. As the singing body adds this layer, the word 'Kollaps' overflows with meaning and is constantly redefined.

Through this approach, music, even when it uses words, detaches itself from the clear-cut representation of language. Each time the listener thinks they might grasp the meaning of the word, Bargeld extends his manifold body into a scream. Much more than a narrated text that appeals to the rational mind, the musical gesture with which the lyrics are delivered touches the ear of the listener. Through the articulation of Bargeld's voice, music uncannily merges with language and emphasizes the sensuous over the intelligible. Keeping with the improvisatory nature of Einstürzende Neubauten's early lyrics, this is not a written text. It is a voice writing in music.

As such, the song 'Kollaps' does not simply tell a story of destruction but sounds like a lament. Alongside the collapsing cities explicitly featured in the text ('We destroy the cities'), the grain inscribed in Bargeld's voice and his fragmenting delivery also invoke the collapse and reconstruction of his own body.[15] With every repetition, the destructive force embedded in the word 'Kollaps' itself seems to tear his body down. And at the same time, Bargeld pulls himself up to push the word out of his lungs. By putting his whole body into his singing, the song becomes the expression of an 'I' that wants to be another. The song is an exorcism, performed to both destroy everything that regulates the body and reinvent it over and over again.

Like Bargeld's voice, music itself is infinitely malleable. It exerts a compelling force because it remains unpredictable. Music, Bargeld posited, 'does not exist unless you have a glimpse of utopia; if it doesn't have that it's not music . . . it has to offer the unthinkable, something beyond language.'[16] In each collapse of music lies its future, because for music to stay alive, it should be relentlessly turned inside out to reconfigure its inner workings. This makes *Kollaps* a life-affirming record: Einstürzende Neubauten used unconventional instruments, played conventional instruments in unconventional ways, discovered unimagined sounds, reconfigured the duration and structure of songs and manipulated the grain of the voice. 'If we can handle all those different things', Bargeld said, 'we could bring the energy point to a stage high enough to bring it to a state of collapse; a final implosion to create black holes! That is my Sehnsucht, my longing. That's the Tanzdebil [*sic*] in me. Siva's dancing! Siva's dancing!'[17] The Hindu deity Siva is known as the destroyer, but also as the cosmic dancer. Dancing the divine dance called Tandava, Siva destroys the world. His dance is a fundamental part of the cycle of creation. You must destroy to build. Music touches upon life because it creates and destroys. It solely exists like this.

Draussen ist Feindlich
Time in the studio

According to the band's official narrative, Einstürzende Neubauten was founded on 1 April 1980, at the Moon Diskothek in Berlin. Origin stories, however, are rarely straightforward. The band name, for instance, already appeared on a cassette recorded in Blixa Bargeld's apartment in Berlin-Schöneberg in late 1979. It features Bargeld and N.U. Unruh (as N-Dih), together with Susä Hobeck and Bettina Köster, both of whom also joined some of the band's earliest live shows.[1] The cassette is credited to the individual musicians and was released in May 1980, around the same time as the first release by Einstürzende Neubauten proper: *Live in Kunstkopfstereo* – a recording of the debut concert at the Moon Diskothek. Both cassettes were released on Eisengrau, Bargeld's own underground tape label named after his shop in the Goltzstrasse in Berlin-Schöneberg that served as a meeting point for the local scene.[2]

Like in so many places around the world in the 1980s, the Berliner underground embraced cassette tapes as the easiest, quickest and most affordable medium to bring often self-recorded and lo-fi music to fans. In quick succession, Eisengrau released small runs of tapes by key artists in the Berliner scene: Die Tödliche Doris, Frieder Butzmann, Alexander von Borsig, Mania D. and Bargeld's own Einstürzende Neubauten.

Following *Live in Kunstkopfstereo*, a second tape called *Chaos → Sehnsucht/Energie* was released in June 1980. It mostly documents the group's second live show on 12 April, in the infamous SO36 club. The first track, however, is a fractured and heavily processed dub mix of 'Fuer den Untergang', here subtitled 'Kriegstanz' (War Dance), recorded by Bargeld and Unruh in a proper recording studio in May. The final mix of this song appeared as the band's debut vinyl single in October 1980.[3]

This constant blending of live shows, cassette releases and studio recordings during the first months of their existence shows that Einstürzende Neubauten's improvisational practice, compositional skills and audience engagement were equally shaped by live performances as they were by recording practices. Even the early live registrations attest to the fact that both recording and performing were instrumental in the development of their sound. Whereas professional live albums attempt to sonically emulate the experience of being-present at the show as much as possible, these lo-fi tapes do not reproduce that experience at all. Because they are produced and reproduced by simple, poor-quality equipment, the rough and muddled sound is an intrinsic part of the music itself.

Such foregrounding of the artificial nature of sound recordings (whether out of necessity or by choice) is a common trait among Eisengrau artists. Their releases showcase a playful experimental approach, characterized by the use of cheap and sometimes partly broken electronic instruments and sound equipment, a love for abstract sound collages and found sounds and a keen ear for simple but compelling sound effects. This free-spirited music thereby highlights one of the basic affordances of sound recording technology: a microphone can turn any sound into music, making it available to use at will, just by recording it and putting it out into the world for curious ears to hear.

Einstürzende Neubauten's *Stahlmusik* cassette, produced in June and released in September 1980, takes full stock of this potential. Created in a single take in a highway underpass, its contents exist somewhere in-between live recording and studio recording. 'Live', because the entire thing was recorded in one take, using an ordinary cassette recorder and making effective use of the hollow sound produced by the room's reverberations. 'The concrete, transforming the noises from outside', writes Klaus Laufer, 'acts as a soothing amplifier . . . Like a thick, felty filter it gives . . . the pleasure of an intense and personal concert'.[4] 'Studio', because of the absence of an audience and the clear artistic choice of using this particular location for the sole purpose of making this specific recording, effectively turning the space into a recording studio. Furthermore, the lo-fi quality of the reproduction audibly emphasizes that this is, and can only be, a recording.

While *Stahlmusik* thereby accentuates how the very act of sound recording turns any location into a studio of sorts, this principle goes both ways: just like the strategic placement of a cassette recorder turned a crawl space in an underpass pillar into a makeshift recording facility, the band turned conventional recording studios into sites for their unorthodox, disruptive performance practices. The *Fuer den Untergang* vinyl single showcases these two approaches. The studio recording on side A is an early example of Einstürzende Neubauten's effective use of minimal means to achieve great impact. The low, thumping resonance of Unruh's drum set is interpolated by swaths of synthesizer noise, and Bargeld's vocals are offset by his piercing guitar screeches. Together, they maintain an impressive sense of urgency throughout the song. On the B-side, however, the 'Stahlversion' of the same song is an outtake of the *Stahlmusik* recording session and, as such, a much more lo-fi rendition. Booming resonance and a thick layer of analogue tape hiss turn it into a rather claustrophobic affair.

Thus, over the course of 1980 and 1981, the band consistently explored the creative interplay between live performance and sound recording. These explorations reached a new high when Bargeld, Unruh and F.M. Einheit, now a trio, entered Hamburg's Hafenklang Studio in April 1981. On the first day of their recording session, the in-house engineer was so shocked by the racket they produced – 'hauling around pieces of steel, everyone screaming, distorted guitars and such' – that he left them to operate a 16-track analogue reel-to-reel tape recorder on their own.[5] As a result, Einheit remembered, they learned 'how a studio works pretty well', just following the basic assumption that if sound 'goes in on one end', it 'should come out again at the other end'.[6] Born out of necessity, this hands-on attitude was fully congruent with the band's approach: like musical instruments or power tools, there is no need to learn how to 'properly' operate a recording studio. The only goal is to generate unexpected sounds and make music that is provocative and thrilling. To get there, everything is permitted.

The result of these April-sessions was the *Kalte Sterne* double 7" single, released in July 1981. It very much functioned as a dry run for *Kollaps*. Although the rhythm section is not yet fully developed, the way the band combines discordant guitars, menacing vocals and whirling synthesizers on its first two tracks matches anything on their debut album. On the next two shorter and more abstract pieces, the band's exploration of the affordances of a recording studio really comes to the fore. These are sound collages rather than band performances, made of spliced tape-loops, clattering drums, jarring guitar chords and Bargeld's screams. The final track, 'Schwarz' (Black), is the most impressive. Backed by droning synthesizer chords and very slow percussive movement, Bargeld delivers a focused, captivating and unsettling vocal performance. 'Don't go', he sings, 'never again/hold me tight/I hold you tight'.[7] This dense, brooding and mysteriously dark love song is the sound of a band coming into its own, finding a unique voice in the studio.

Like *Kalte Sterne*, *Kollaps* was recorded over the course of several weeks without a producer or engineer. The entire album was written, performed, recorded and mixed by those three men in that same studio in Hamburg. Left to their own devices, they took matters into their own hands and became performers, sound engineers and record producers in one, approaching each role like they did everything: idiosyncratic, exploratory and without respecting established rules or norms. All one needs to know about sound recording is that sound goes in at one end and comes out at the other.

In between the two ends, however, is where things get interesting, because along its journey from input to output, from sender to receiver, sound is affected by the physical characteristics of the machines, cables and effect boxes through which it travels. All these devices and objects leave a mark on the signal and thereby shape the specific *sound* of whatever it is that is being transmitted, recorded and reproduced. Rather than thinking of sound recordings as derivatives of live performances, it therefore makes more sense to think of recorded music as something entirely different. Because the channels between input and output change the sounds they capture and transmit, what happens on one end and comes out at the other are not two versions of the same sound event. Instead, the end result of a recording process, the finished record, is a unique and singular performance in and of itself.

In the work of Einstürzende Neubauten, this fundamental difference between live performance and sound recording had been clear from the beginning, because neither one functioned as the primary site of their musical production. The band began recording as soon as they began playing live, and these recordings were not just faithfully reproducing performances, nor were the performances staging previously recorded material. The physical properties of the recording equipment and crucial factors like the types of microphones that were used, where they were placed and the acoustics of the room affect the sound so drastically that the experience of listening to the cassettes is incomparable to attending the live shows. The recorded performance thereby becomes something entirely separate from the initial live performance.

The consecutive recording sessions for *Kalte Sterne* and *Kollaps* thoroughly explored these musical possibilities of recording technology. They document how three restlessly creative people learned to operate a recording studio in real-time and discovered the limitless artistic potential of technological sound manipulation. Through the power of transduction, each and every sound can be captured and turned into electrical signals. As such, it can be amplified, filtered, distorted, reversed, cut and combined at will. Even more poignantly, contact microphones can directly transduce all vibrating surfaces into electricity and thereby turn all kinds of objects into potential sources of sound production. This way, for instance, the clips that attach microphones to mic-stands provide the plucking sound on 'Negativ Nein'. And the bangs on Unruh's metal drum kit in 'Tanz Debil' are filtered to such an extent that its overtones produce rudimental melodic figures throughout the song.

With this autodidactic takeover of the studio, Einstürzende Neubauten repurposed the feverish improvisational energy of their live performances to fit the more exploratory nature of sound recording. 'Einstürz-Ende [*sic*] Neubauten in the studio', Einheit described,

> means two, three nights without sleep, to work through, to give your best, come closer to insanity; means Hans Rosenthal and Ronald Reagan in Dachau accompanied by the Trinidad Steel Band at the peak of their cold turkey. Batteries of short-circuited transistor radios and television sets, sweat and the erotic.[8]

In other words, just as they subverted the concept and practices of a 'band' performing on 'stage', they subverted the concept of a 'band' recording music in a 'studio', relentlessly scratching at the extremes of human experience. Using the same exploratory trial-and-error approach that defined their live improvisations, the band's idiosyncratic production choices firmly position the music away from the stage and in the space of the recording studio.

On 'Steh auf Berlin', for instance, the cleanly recorded metal drumming is interpolated by sudden bursts of close mic-ed noise, and the limping beat in 'Schmerzen Hören' is abruptly cut off after two and a half minutes to immediately transition into the shrill keyboard sound of 'Jet'm'. Achieving similar levels of immediacy and ferocity as they did on stage, but by very different means, Bargeld called this approach 'guerrilla tactics as recording strategy'.[9] It means they constantly pushed the limits of what seemed possible and put things together that did not seem to fit.

An important musical touchstone for this approach to record production is the techniques developed by dub-producers in Jamaica in the late 1960s and early 1970s. Not so much a genre as a musical attitude to sound, dub can be regarded as one of the most influential developments in the history of popular music. Pioneered by the increasingly experimental sound manipulations of reggae producers like King Tubby and Lee 'Scratch' Perry, dub's way of mixing records redefined what recorded music is or can be. Instead of aiming for a well-balanced mix of various instrumental parts, these producers used studio techniques such as extreme equalization, artificial reverberation, combining different types of echo and delay effects, the sudden removal or introduction of instrumental parts, and applying noise gates or phase effects to create abstract, otherworldly instrumental arrangements.[10]

Many of the production choices heard on *Kollaps* are indebted to dub-techniques.[11] Throughout 'U-Haft Muzak' and

'Abstieg & Zerfall' (Descent & Decay), for instance, instrumental elements are panned to the extreme left and right of the stereo image, while different types of natural and artificial reverb put each of those elements in their own distinctive acoustic space. Similarly, on 'Negativ Nein' (Negative No), the two main elements of the song – a dry, repetitive, plucking motive and Bargeld's delayed and distorted screams – occupy disparate acoustic spaces. The influence of dub is most audible, however, in the way the band treats the rhythm section. In 1982, they even released a series of dub-mixes called *Stahldubversions* (Steel Dub Versions), many of which are essentially brief and rudimentary templates for the rhythmic groundwork of songs on *Kollaps*.[12]

On a more conceptual level, the sound manipulations of dub music can also be understood as a way to, as musician and sound scholar David Toop puts it, sonically 'displace time, shift the beat, heighten a mood, suspend a moment'.[13] As a fundamentally temporal art form, the relation between sound and time has always been a defining feature of music, but the introduction of recording technology offered a whole new set of tools to explore this age-old relationship. Capturing transient sound events and storing them on hardware carriers, as sound recording does, enabled new ways to repeat, displace, stretch, reverse and compress sound. It allowed musicians and composers to use the manipulation of sound to explicitly tinker with the listener's experience of time, which is what dub is all about.

By explicitly putting the experience of time through music to the fore, the kinds of production techniques used on *Kollaps* further emphasize a fundamental feature of the act of sound recording itself: like any act of storage and record keeping (from writing to painting and from bookkeeping to memorizing an epic poem), it attempts to capture moments in time that would otherwise be lost. In other words, it tries to hold on to the past. Whereas the act of performance reaches out into the world in the spur of the moment and interacts with its chaotic, unpredictable and ever-changing splendour, the act of recording captures, closes in, contains, holds on to and encloses the world. Recorded music thereby offers listeners a way to experience the moment as it unfolds in time, while simultaneously grappling with its fundamental transience in a more sustained way.

Following this line of reasoning, *Kollaps* is a dispatch, sent out into the world and across space and time from that recording studio in Hamburg in the summer of 1981. It contains the sound of three men, sleepless and tirelessly working to store all their explosive energy on magnetic tape. Instead of trying to reproduce the urgency and vitalism of their live performances and freeze them in time, they turned their recorded music into something else entirely. By stretching, manipulating and compressing sound, they put it outside of the regular flow of time. Locked in the studio, away from the stage, the audience and the hostile world outside, they call to us, their listeners, and try to reach us by all means. *Kollaps* is an invitation to join them, as Bargeld whispers in our ears: 'shut yourself in with me . . . here we are safe'.[14]

Negativ Nein
The love of noise

Kollaps, or so the story goes, was intended to be unlistenable.
And to this date, reviewers and commentators still frequently
repeat or confirm it is.[1] Surely, the album is not easy-listening.
Over forty years after its release, its stark sounds and lyrical
imagery keep challenging unsuspecting listeners. N.U. Unruh,
however, does not think 'the record is unlistenable' at all, nor
does he remember a deliberate plan to make it so.[2] And he
is right, of course, because what does 'unlistenable' mean,
anyway? Anyone with a functioning set of ears can listen to
the record. Only when the volume is cranked up to ten, it
might become physically unpleasant. But then again, so does
playing a Mozart string quartet at an incredibly loud volume.
'Unlikeable' or maybe 'unloveable' might be more accurate
terms, but they still belie the longevity and influence of the
album. Most importantly, all these qualifications ignore the
basic observation that the music is actually liked, loved and
listened by generations of fans. It speaks to them, appeals
to them and touches them. *Kollaps*, like any music, is not
unlistenable, unlikeable or unloveable at all.

What is more, the supposedly 'unlistenable'
experimentalism of Einstürzende Neubauten's music was not
without precedent. Even if we limit our view to the Western

world, by 1980, composers like Edgard Varèse, Iannis Xenakis, Pierre Schaeffer and others had been experimenting with electronic music for decades, with results that are often equally dense and complex, or much more so. Likewise, the free jazz developed from the 1950s onward in the United States by composers like Ornette Coleman, Cecil Taylor or Sun Ra exploded conventional concepts of improvisation. And in the late 1970s, the abrasive work of Throbbing Gristle and other acts in the British 'industrial music'-scene drew inspiration from a wide range of artistic, musical, literary and countercultural sources to set new standards for harsh and extreme performances. Some years before, in 1975, Lou Reed released *Metal Machine Music* (1975), an album featuring over an hour of guitar feedback and noise effects that Unruh often listened to.[3]

All in all, the whole idea of an 'unlistenable' record might have been nothing but an effective marketing ploy by the band itself: an audacious anti-establishment statement to solidify the group's rapidly spreading reputation. Bargeld admitted as much when he said that he would only 'call Neubauten's stuff noise . . . for the sake of simplicity'.[4] His real concern, he confessed, was not to make off-putting music but to make music that genuinely related to his 'attitude and . . . situation in life'.[5] In other words, he wanted to make music that could reflect life in West-Berlin in the early 1980s, where economic hardship and nuclear threat fed the prevailing sense of impending doom. Rather than just 'being unlistenable' for the sake of it, then, the harsher, more challenging aspects of Einstürzende Neubauten's music reflect these very particular historical and socio-economic circumstances that the band members found themselves in. The record is as unlistenable as West-Berlin was unliveable.

Confronted with the indelibly tainted and suspect history of German culture, the band touted the seemingly radical idea of the 'destruction of music' to forge a clean slate. Rather than the complete eradication or annihilation of the concept of music, however, this destruction encompassed their attempt to subvert all established categories of 'music' by collapsing the difference between apparent opposites: pleasant and unpleasant, skilled and unskilled, musical and unmusical, beautiful and repulsive, listenable and unlistenable, sound and noise. Einstürzende Neubauten wanted to subvert whatever people expect of music and expand the notion of music itself in the process. To get rid of the idea that certain sounds, objects, gestures or ideas are musical and others are not, the band consistently pushed the boundaries of what 'music' was considered to be. They were, as Bargeld put it, 'stretching the frontier until there is nothing left that is not music'.[6] By approaching it like this, they emphasized features of music that usually remain hidden beneath more commonplace parameters like harmony and melody.

Bargeld's dislike for the term notwithstanding, the most effective way to label these hidden features is, indeed, 'noise'. Noise, however, is a multifaceted concept that means many different things. Einstürzende Neubauten's music is commonly associated with the most mundane use of the term, signifying 'loud' or 'disruptive' sound, or, more broadly, anything that does not fit standard concepts of music. Already in nineteenth-century physical acoustics, this concept of unstructured or chaotic 'noise' was pitted against the ideal of structured and well-ordered musical 'sound'. To this day, this supposed difference between musical *sound* and unmusical *noise* remains common in everyday discourses on sound and music. It is exactly the kind of supposedly clear-cut opposition that the band wanted to get rid of.

Alongside this understanding of 'noise' in opposition to 'sound' and 'music', however, the meaning and understanding of the term were significantly expanded in the late nineteenth and early twentieth centuries with the introduction of communication media like the telephone, gramophone and telegraph; and even more so with the development of computational information technologies after the Second World War. With the emergence of these technological paradigms, engineers and information theorists identified noise as an inherent feature of signal transmission and an unavoidable and even necessary presence in all communication channels. Following communication and information theory, noise is not the opposite of sound but always already a part of it. In a musical context, this means it is not an extramusical element (an intrusion or disruption) but a musical parameter as important as rhythm, melody and harmony. The rich sonority of metal banging, the clatter of jackhammer drilling and the discordant chords of untuned guitars do not destroy or disrupt. They expand the domain of music.

Furthermore, this twentieth-century communicational or informational concept of noise also reinforced the inseparable connection between the sounds of music and the media channels that transmit these sounds. In physical terms, a sound signal requires some kind of medium (or channel) to be

transmitted and heard: a soothing voice, a ferociously played violin or a delicately beaten steel plate all produce vibrations in the medium 'air' that our ears pick up and our brains process as 'sound'. Significantly, all these sounds contain random, irregular or 'noisy' elements that are the result of their material production and transmission. Resonating wood boards or metal plates, vibrating strings or membranes and air flows pushed through a narrow tube do not just produce well-rounded, harmonious 'tones', but also highly specific, irregular vibrations that define the specific quality, or timbre of sounds. In short, the material shapes the sound.

A microphone, in turn, registers acoustic air pressure and transduces it into electrical current, and a loudspeaker turns these electrical signals back into moving air. On top of the noisy elements produced by the acoustic production of a sound, the material characteristics of these devices and all interlinking plugs, cables, membranes, tubes and transistors used to transmit, transform and store recorded sound add their own particular noisy characteristics and thereby change the acoustic character of the sound as well.

So, although sound media can indiscriminately capture and reproduce everything that sounds (whether traditionally 'musical' or not at all), they also change and shape its acoustic properties – the specific *sound* of each sound – in the process. Because of this, these technologies quickly became tools for exploring uncharted musical territories. On *Kollaps*, this results in extraordinary riches: from the sound of drumming on junkyard items to overloaded screams and hushed, close-mic'd whispers, from discordant guitar jangles and thumping pneumatic drills to field recordings and found tape footage,

from eerie synthesizer chords to bubbling water bottles. By putting all these irregular and contingent sounds front and centre, the band exposes the unavoidable but often ignored noise-elements that are inherent to the material production and reproduction of each and every sound.

The very first sound on *Kollaps* is the soft crackling of what appears to be a malfunctioning amplifier. Next comes a buzzing synthesizer chord. Seemingly insignificant, but purposefully placed, these opening seconds announce the importance of noise on the album. In the world of Einstürzende Neubauten, everything, from household objects to steel plates, from hammers and power tools to radio and TV sets, from synthesizers to electric guitars, can be used as sound-generating device: 'the song sleeps in the machine.'[7]

So, in discussing this music, 'noise' does not – or not only – refer to the heavily compressed drumming on 'Tanz Debil' or the jackhammer-metal-on-metal assault of 'Steh auf Berlin'. In fact, these moments of full-on cacophony are not all that prominent on the album. The sounds that truly shape the music and draw the listener in are the crackles, the whirrs and the static, the buzzing, scraping and whispering – soft sounds that do not hide the material basis of their production. Surprisingly often, *Kollaps* is quiet, subdued, stark and depleted. The final song on the album, 'Helga', is just eight seconds of found radio footage, after which it resolves into silence.

Of course, at times, the music is loud, menacing, even violent, but for every such outburst, there is a quieter, more introspective moment. Sometimes, the tone changes abruptly. After the raucous clamour of the first two songs, the first thirty

seconds of 'Negativ Nein' contain nothing but the sound of bubbling water and a brief plucked melody. The calm is interrupted by Blixa Bargeld's scream, but this melodic motive remains his sole accompaniment throughout the remainder of the song. Next, the desolate sound of 'U-Haft Muzak' relies almost entirely on well-placed noise textures – static, buzzing, scraping, crackling – that interpolate a thumping, slow-paced and slightly limping beat. Similarly, the drumming on 'Schmerzen Hören' is slow, simple and not noisy at all. The song's intensity is produced by Bargeld's shouting, combined with sudden bursts of feedback that are brief but loud. By contrasting the uniform rhythmic basis, this combination of noise bursts and more subdued sounds propels the music forward.

This back-and-forth between chaos and order, contingency and control as the main drivers of musical tension makes noise itself a productive force.[8] Alongside well-ordered, controllable and therefore predictable sounds and structures, noise allows for unexpected and surprising outcomes. It creates musical potential. This principle lies at the heart of Einstürzende Neubauten's art, down to the double-sidedness of their band name. Just like the addition of a dose of noise threatens to overtake or derail a structured piece of music, the collapse of a building might constitute the definitive endpoint of a well-ordered architectural structure, but the resulting chaos and disarray also offer unexpected possibilities for other arrangements of the same material – different structures and new buildings.

Rather than unpleasant or off-putting, the 'noise' on *Kollaps* is therefore 'a positive sound', as Bargeld has it.[9] 'Negativ nein!'

he shouts on the eponymous song: Negative? No! The product of two negatives is a positive, or even 'the most positive of all possibilities'.[10] Similarly, noise's undoing of order plants a seed for creation. It is the positively life-affirming force behind the band's music. It does not reject or confront the listener but, like the physical intensity of the band's stage performances, forges a connection. Noise reaches out across the distance and touches the listeners, inviting them to come closer and listen more intimately. To listen so intensely that it hurts. To listen with pain.

Take 'Abstieg & Zerfall', the second-to-last track on the album. It opens with a plucked guitar chord, followed by the clacking sound of a switch. A buzzing synthesizer sets in, and the sound of feedback and metal scraping begins. In the first fifty seconds before the rhythm track and vocals join in, the music is measured and restrained, but the nervous anticipation is palpable. The hesitantly plucked guitar and the click of the switch function like opening a door: the listener crosses a threshold and steps into the song. The careful positioning of complex timbres and rough textures subsequently builds and maintains the musical tension. Noise is the connector, the medium of choice. Without it, there would be no music, no message and no relation.

The title track, opening side B of the vinyl record, is by far the longest and perhaps the most straightforward song on the album, with identifiable verses and an almost sing-along chorus. Its main body is built around one ringing guitar chord, struck over and over again and backed by a rudimental, propulsive rhythm. Throughout, Bargeld repeats different iterations of the word *Kollaps*. This main section is flanked, however, by a full minute of whirling feedback and synthesizer noise at the beginning of the track and a sudden breakdown into dissonant tones and gut-wrenching screams at the end. The rhythmic, melodic and harmonic immediacy of the main tune is thereby offset by the racket in its opening and closing sections. The noise at the beginning sets the tone and shapes the mood. The shrill disruption at the end breaks the spell and shuts the door. Noise, in short, invites you in and kicks you out.

Used like this, as an inherent part of musical communication, noise is not incidental, external or anti-musical. On the contrary, it is elementary, unavoidable and essential. As French philosopher Michel Serres writes:

> We are surrounded by noise. And this noise is inextinguishable. It is outside – it is the world itself – and it is inside, produced by our living body. We are in the noises of the world, we cannot close our door to their reception, and we evolve, rolling in this incalculable swell.[11]

Noise, Serres confirms, is not a negative intruder but a positive affirmation, because it is intrinsic to the functioning of the ever-changing natural world outside and of our own living and decaying body. It is all around and inside. Still, in former times, it was regularly expelled from the realm of music by strict regimes of harmony and melody that created a deceptive sense of order and security. On *Kollaps*, the rehabilitation of the irregular, chaotic and unpredictable side of sound therefore binds the music to the irregular, chaotic and unpredictable world outside.

By embodying the complexity of the world, the noise of *Kollaps* is essential to the way the music speaks to its audience. It is fundamentally relational and key to Einstürzende Neubauten's attempt to make contact by all means necessary. Through its use, they extend an invitation to come together and enter into a relationship – to form a community of musicians and listeners. 'Come here', it says, emphatically, 'come with us', join in, 'shut yourself in with me', come together, 'listen to my wounds'. The affective quality of noise allows the musicians to reach out and establish a connection. It is a way to get up close, as it were, and almost physically touch the listener.

In the end, the most positive undercurrent in Einstürzende Neubauten's music – the most positive of all possibilities – might therefore just be: *love*. The attentive listener, who accepts the invitation and takes up the challenge, finds a record full of love in unexpected places. Beyond all the racket, the screaming, the banging, the destructive imagery and the seeming negativity, *Kollaps* deals with longing and desire. It is a plea for communality, intimacy, tenderness and sensitivity. Case in point is the very last song on side A – right before the listener had to reach out, grab the vinyl record, and flip it over: 'Jet'm' – *je t'aime* . . .

enticing song of beauty. Instantly recognizable, it is the only melody on Einstürzende Neubauten's debut album that can rightly be called catchy. It lingers in the head of the listener, especially because of the silence that follows after the close of side A. As involuntary as love occupies the mind, 'Jet'm' remains an earworm. This deceptive cadence of *Kollaps'* first half thereby leaves the listener with a completely different impression than its exposition suggested.

'Jet'm' thereby offers an opening towards a different kind of music. The empty space that breaks the record in two is filled with all the possible directions it might take from there on. After this familiar melody, it suddenly becomes much more uncertain what might be in store for the remainder of the album. By its mere presence, love shimmers through on *Kollaps*. Not only in 'Jet'm' itself, but for the record as a whole. A hidden quality, maybe even forbidden, but always present. Love is at its centre.

More than just a throwaway cover version or simple homage, 'Jet'm' is one of the main building blocks of *Kollaps*. Lifted from its original context, the melody functions like a citation, not to make a point, but to express love as a universal truth. For philosopher Walter Benjamin, a citation, in the literary sense, 'summons the word by its name, wrenches it destructively from its context, but precisely thereby calls it back to its origin'.[4] To cite, for Benjamin, therefore means to go back to the roots of a word, to a language that connects us to the world. By disclosing this language, citations circumvent historical conditions. As such, citing is a process of discovery. It unveils things that were lost over the course of history.

Accordingly, with 'Jet'm', Einstürzende Neubauten uncover something contained in the melody of 'Je t'aime . . . moi non plus', namely the love expressed by the original. Gainsbourg's song did not fit traditional values and was banned, because it was a visceral love song. The citation recognizes and uses this potential. By leaving the melody intact and quoting it in full, it infuses *Kollaps* with an energy that could not be expressed otherwise.

Although it might have been more logical for the band to take an equally suitable citation closer to home, for instance, sourced from the nineteenth-century tradition of German Romanticism, this was not possible, because, as Bargeld explained, 'there was no German tradition one could refer to without feeling guilty. That culture which existed before the war is rightly forbidden to us, because of what it led to – or at best, did not prevent'.[5] Love, as a part of German culture, was cut off from its origin, and to retrieve it, Einstürzende Neubauten had to wrench it from the past and claim it back. By looking for it in places other than their own background, they could leave tradition behind, while still incorporating a universal element of love into their own work.

They were able to do so because, as Benjamin specifies, citations have 'the power not to preserve but to purify, to tear from context, to destroy'.[6] Which is to say, preservation is conservative. It safeguards traditional values and prevents the past from becoming part of the present, except as a relic – a consecrated and untouchable object. Preservation relinquishes the past. Purification, by contrast, removes the historical situatedness in search of an intrinsic quality contained in the citation. By transporting it to the present, what is cited is no longer historically stymied but becomes part of a contemporary practice. It breathes new life into the past. This way, Einstürzende Neubauten salvage love as a viable force in their own music. They might have lived amidst the rubble of a city in which the apocalypse was a constant threat, but they cherished love as an intrinsic part of life. By cutting 'Jet'm' into their record, the band nurtured love and carved out a space for it to dwell in.

'Quotations', writes Benjamin, 'are like wayside robbers who leap out, armed, and relieve the idle stroller of his conviction'.[7] Indeed, after having heard the first six songs of *Kollaps*, the melody quoted in 'Jet'm' takes the listener by surprise. As a citation, it emphasizes that there is always a relation between the act of destruction and that which it inherently uncovers. As such, the melody calls all ideas about the record that listeners formed up to that point into question. 'Jet'm' might therefore be the most subversive song on *Kollaps*, because it subverts the record itself from the inside. With their interpretation of Gainsbourg, Einstürzende Neubauten undermined their own destructive impulses. Brief as it might be, 'Jet'm' is a declaration of love to music, but rather than using words that sing about love, they name it with music.

'Jet'm', however, does not just simply bring to mind Gainsbourg's *histoire d'amour*. After all, besides sentimental moods, love is a disruptive force. It sweeps all rationality aside in the blink of an eye. 'Kollaps', the contrasting next song, on the other side of the record, is testament to this devastation that love can provoke: 'burn me/tear me down, down, again and again'.[8] With its tremendous force, it says, love tells you that something is about to change. Felt so intensely that it does not keep track of restrictions or common values. It is not just a feeling. Love acts in the name of difference. Its desire for the other, love shares with music.

When Bargeld came across a record of Ethiopian music, he was not only impressed by the raw grain in the singing voice, the clapping as rhythmic accompaniment and the ingenuity of the self-made instruments.[9] More fundamentally, through this music, he experienced sound unburdened by prior musical knowledge. It opened his ears to the immeasurable potential of sound and its possibilities for creating music. He discovered a genuine love for music as such, which inspired him to enter into a relationship with music not based on tradition or modelled on familiar systems of communication but rooted in the creative potential of each and every sound. He recognized this potential because he heard something outside of the ordinary. When it is not restricted by any notions of type or form or genre, music as a whole is polyphonic. It can be whatever you want it to be.[10]

For Einstürzende Neubauten, this realization provided an antidote for the stale state that music had reached for them: a predictable accumulation of sound, as if the constant repetition of similar sounding music exhausted the breathable air. It meant a break with music as a product of neoliberal consumerism. 'What worked in the desert', Bargeld recalls the music of the Ethiopian nomads, 'would work in the urban environment on the debris of consumer society as well'.[11]

Other than the Ethiopian desert, however, making music in West-Berlin in the early 1980s came with the burden of German history and the traditions of Western music. On several occasions, Bargeld therefore referred to *The Destructive Character*, a short piece by Benjamin.[12] Much more than a philosophy, technique or theory, this text describes a relationship to the world similar in many ways to the purifying impulse Benjamin found in citations. The 'destructive character', he writes, makes room and 'clears away the traces of our own age'.[13] For Einstürzende Neubauten, to make room for the kind of free and unburdened music they wanted to make, this meant they had to dissolve the traces of their own musical tradition altogether.[14]

As a result, while making *Kollaps,* Einstürzende Neubauten started over and over again with every song, trying to hear sound afresh and invent music that would be just as new. The destructive character rejuvenates and almost returns music to a paradisal origin, albeit one that remains impossible to know or reconstruct in full: a music devoid of history, sound heard for the first time as music. By using sounds that communicate nothing but themselves, however, the songs on *Kollaps* do reach back to this primordial quality of music. As each one exists in its own singular auditory world, sounds appear as if heard for the first time, stripped of all historical connotations and values that music absorbed over the years. The songs thereby try to attain what music might be, if it were untainted by tradition.

This goal is not as unattainable as it might seem, as long as music is not considered to be limited. It is not. Music is a limitless entity that offers a constant renewal of combinations of sounds and an equally unlimited variety of listening experiences. Music that honours this limitless quality, like the music on *Kollaps*, allows for a listening experience that rejuvenates the love for music itself. This is the origin and foundation of Einstürzende Neubauten, and its mentality is the destructive character. The destructive character surpasses tradition and thereby reclaims the full potential of music.

Time and time again, *Kollaps* is mistakenly seen as an aggressive record, because the fierceness of a love for singular musical experiences is perceived as destructive. But it is not a violent record. It is not even that loud. It is out of the ordinary, in the strictest sense of what was perceived customary in 1981. *Kollaps* was, however, necessary to return music to a space where expectations are set aside. A place where every act of listening is a confrontation with something extraordinary. What music evokes can be astonishing, bewildering or even devastating, and the more unpredictable it is, the deeper the mark that music inscribes. 'Jet'm', as a symbol of love, is the sound of music's awakening.

Sehnsucht
Desire

Kollaps closes with thirty seconds of silence. Not, however, just with the absence of music but with a singular silence that belongs to this record only. In these final moments, the body throbs. After a dance of creation and destruction, blood gushes through veins and nerves crackle with electricity. What remains after a collapse is a moment of trembling contemplation, when dust settles, panic subsides and a heaving body recovers. The first discernible sound will be a breath: a sigh that signifies the desire to live.

This silence takes up around three quarters of the final track, 'Helga'.[1] Right before, a woman's voice, heavily distorted by radio or television noise, says: 'Unfortunately, youthful commitment, individual, personal commitment is blocked to this day by propaganda, namely by negative propaganda.' This can be read as a critique of the one-dimensionality of music as a commodity item. Everything that is unique and out of line seems to disappear from the sphere of the audible, swamped by the masses of musics that represent nothing but uniformity. Sometimes, however, young musicians stray from the beaten path. With a rumbling noise, they steer into different directions to interrogate musical conformity.

The words from 'Helga' nearly become inaudible amidst the hiss, almost as if this youthful commitment, both individual and personal, is indeed unwelcome, like a noise, repressed by society. Like noise, however, these disturbances always resurface because they grow and come from within. Such was, for instance, the case with jazz music in the first half of the twentieth century. Noise, persistent as life itself, found a place in and through jazz, where it could thrive and not be silenced.[2] Noise is more than loudness. It is also the act of improvisation itself, as it disrupts the very system from within. In jazz, order only exists to be annulled. And at the same time, improvisation is an indispensable, defining element, because it weaves the music together.

Even if it happens for just a moment, played by a soloist or collectively, each and every improvisation leads away from the current music towards other musical regions. On *Kollaps,* the song 'Vorm Krieg' (Before the War), for instance, directs the ears towards music outside of the record itself. These twenty seconds of compressed jazz – a collage made of fragments from 'Sweet Marijuana Brown' by the Barney Bigard Sextet – remind us that the noise of youthful individual expression might as well be a spark that ignites the flame of music once again.[3]

This movement from one type of music towards another is like wandering in the night to unheard places. On 'Kollaps', Blixa sings, 'Our odysseys / destroy the cities / and nocturnal wandering / levels them to the ground.'[4] Printed above the lyrics to the song in the record's booklet is a drawing of a little monster with the caption 'nächtliches Wandern' (nocturnal wandering). The figure is just two lumpy legs and a filled-out black circle, like a head without an eye or other facial features. It cannot see, but it might have the faculty of hearing to orient itself in the dark. This image and its resonances in the lyrics recall the ideal of wandering that was a central motive in nineteenth-century German Romanticism. From the music of Franz Schubert and Robert Schumann to the poems of Friedrich Hölderlin and Johann Wolfgang von Goethe and, perhaps most famously, Caspar David Friedrich's painting *Der Wanderer über dem Nebelmeer* (The Wanderer above the Mist, 1818).

In Friedrich's painting, a man stands tall on a mountain cliff, looking out over a sea of fog. His destination is in front of him. Although the spectator looks at him on the back, his posture suggests courage: this man does not fear what lies ahead. As he gazes into the distance, the only thing staring back is the unknown. Similar to the painting, what we see in the record's booklet might be the little monster's back, perhaps looking over the ruins of a city. Locked in by the Berlin Wall, Einstürzende Neubauten's nocturnal wanderer has not much space to roam. The little monster is there, though, shrivelled into this little lump, courageous and ready to venture into uncharted territory.

Wandering has a single destination, as the closing lines of Schubert's song *Der Wanderer* suggest: 'And always the sigh asks, where? / It sounds back to me in the spirit's breath: / "There, where you are not, there is happiness".[5] Wandering is a pursuit, not necessarily for an encounter with happiness but for the possibilities that lie wherever you are not. It corresponds to the character of the unknown: the awakening of overwhelming possibilities. How close the destination may be, the wanderer always strives to reach the place where he is not yet. Wandering feeds on desire, which similarly strives outwards. As such, it is intimately related to a central concept in Einstürzende Neubauten's work: *Sehnsucht*.

For a band set to discover new musical territories, the song 'Sehnsucht' sounds oddly old-fashioned. Built around the repetitive touch of a single piano note, the constant tapping of the instrument's timbre brings to mind the history of nineteenth-century piano literature. Still, the song denies the instrument its virtuoso capabilities. Throughout the song, the note is supported by a few chords and the ghostly presence of a synthesizer. 'Sehnsucht' almost seems to be an etude in the German Lied tradition. Its subject matter supports this interpretation.

The lyrics contain just a few words: 'Desire / desire / comes out of chaos / desire / desire / is the only energy / my desire / my addiction / desire / is the only energy'.[6] Blixa Bargeld highlights the words' ambivalence when he sings: 'Meine Sehnsucht / meine Sucht' (my desire / my addiction). Although *Sehnsucht* is often translated as 'desire', the English word does not fully cover its manifold meanings. It is one of those infamous untranslatable words, because it dwells in a dimension of its own, filled with layers of connotations. Contained in the first part of the word is the verb *sehnen*, which means to desire, as well as *Sehne*, the noun for tendons. *Suchen* means searching or striving, while *Sucht* as a noun refers to an irresistible urge. A sickness even, as it also means addiction, obsession and mania. Lastly, the brothers Grimm's *German Dictionary* suggests an etymological relation between the urgent desire of *Sucht* and the word 'sigh', indicating a connection between desire and the vitality of breathing.[7] Consequently, *Sehnsucht* is not just a feeling or an emotion, but a force that acts. It is a type of desire that strives towards the prolongation of life by extending outwards, like a breath.[8] Finally, *Sehnsucht* can also be translated by the English 'craving' or 'longing', which suggests a productive energy searching to elongate itself. *Sehnsucht*, as such, is a sickness, because it tries to escape its own origin and strives to persevere outside of itself, by forging connections beyond itself.[9]

'Sehnsucht' is very different from the preceding song, 'Kollaps'. In the latter, Bargeld sings about collapsing cities, as if the structure of music itself comes crashing down. After this chaos, 'Sehnsucht' offers a more contemplative moment. Precisely because of the remains left behind by the collapse on 'Kollaps', 'Sehnsucht' can follow: 'desire comes out of chaos', sings Bargeld. We find ourselves in a wasteland where some things still stir. Throughout the song, as the repetitive piano note makes a crescendo, the intensity of 'Sehnsucht' grows. 'Kollaps' may have left music in ruins, but the record is far from over. There are five more songs to come. 'Desire is the only energy', asserts Bargeld; it is the force that prolongs the record and propels it forward. 'Sehnsucht' leads into unknown territory, as we are wandering among the ruins of music itself.

Desire sets the music free. Paradoxically, Einstürzende Neubauten's record thrives because the band constantly cuts itself loose from its own music. They even seem to do so after each and every song on *Kollaps*, like when the title track ends and the longing sigh of 'Sehnsucht' brings its much-needed relief. The serenity, however, is not a moment of solace. As the second half of the record continues, it becomes more and more difficult to anticipate what will come next. Especially after the fragmented jazz of 'Vorm Krieg', the impression of a music that stretches out in each and every possible direction can hardly be ignored. The steady sawing movement of 'Hirnsäge' (Brain Saw) makes way for an unexpected ending: the organ sound of 'Abstieg & Zerfall' presents a very different atmosphere than on the first songs on the album. Whereas the record begins with a frontal attack on unsuspecting ears – loud, bright and harsh – the opening sounds shout out to be heard, this second-to-last song is far more ominous. Its billowing feedback has no direction, nor does the organ drone work towards a discernible climax. The sounds haunt and imbue 'Abstieg & Zerfall' with a lingering quality.

These songs at the end of the record are not loud. Metal no longer defines their character. They do not have that same timbral brightness, that ringing in the ear. No more jackhammers or banging metal-on-metal. Instead of clamour and screams, instead of energy crescendoing, comes a more subdued music. If the album were a metal factory, this is the foundry or the smelting furnace. Here, Einstürzende Neubauten are forging new alloys. This music is an ode to difference. It nurtures change.

Desire, as an elementary part of the work, enables these necessary mutations. Its energy is preserved, not through conservation but through limitless transformation. Music must mutate to stay alive, and for Einstürzende Neubauten, desire is the force that diverts from mainstream music towards other possibilities. *Kollaps* is a refusal to make music that already exists. The record does not cling to a city or a world in distress because the music stretches out beyond its own borders. *Kollaps* is a blueprint for a boundless music.

Desire is the breath that fuels life and connects the inside of the living body to the world outside. Air spreads around in the depths of the lungs, where it branches out. Oxygen flows through blood and brains until it is used up and residual gas is exhaled to make room. Just like this, Einstürzende Neubauten feeds itself with sound. The band is an organism that mutates with each consecutive song. It inhales sound. It lives on sound. Just as every breath is an extension of life, sound is Einstürzende Neubauten's sustenance.

This way, the band absorbs other kinds of music and makes certain elements their own. There is, for example, a connection between the ferocity of punk and the song 'Tanz Debil'; undoubtedly 'Jet'm' reminds anyone familiar with Jane Birkin or Serge Gainsbourg of the original; although much rawer and less chiming, 'Draussen ist Feindlich' contains a hint of gamelan;[10] 'Vorm Krieg' recalls jazz as well as the playful found objects of Dada artists; the obstinate repetition of 'Kollaps' has a distinct mantric quality that propels forward, like the drive supporting a Krautrock song; throughout the album, Bargeld's voice expectorates a vocal grain discerned in the music of the Ethiopian Nomads; 'Abstieg & Zerfall' unearths a glooming atmosphere similar to 'Der Leiermann', the last song of Schubert's song cycle *Winterreise*; 'Helga', finally, echoes the overflowing silences of John Cage.

With each song, Einstürzende Neubauten wanders further into unknown territory and encounters different sounds and music to reorganize themselves. It is almost as if *Kollaps* is a book of etudes, a collection of musical rehearsal pieces. They study musical connections, structures and relationships between all the sounds they encounter and long to use. Every song on the album is a further mutation of Einstürzende Neubauten's music and extends their capabilities. *Kollaps* is the musical manifestation of their desire to break free.

Desire is addictive. Its seductive quality leads away from everything one knows and offers unknown worlds in return. This is the point where desire and music converge, because they both unlock untrodden paths. *Kollaps* wanders through a variety of musics and concludes in the silence of 'Helga', where music as such can no longer be easily defined. Silence, though, always has the potential to grow into music. This is the seductive quality of the domain of the audible. Silence draws you in and leads you astray.

Youthful, individual and personal commitment are banned from society. These are the last words on *Kollaps*. In the accompanying booklet, however, a handwritten sentence is added: 'The proof of my positive thinking is your birth!!!'[11] Unspoken, this sentence resonates in the intimate silence that ends the record. Sound may be absent, but this contemplative moment does have something to say. Or rather, it has already been said, not solely through shouting, but sometimes with a delicate whisper: music changes.

Desire extends beyond its place of origin and brings about ruin and decay, because it creates. For Einstürzende Neubauten, it is the energy that shapes music. 'Helga' turns inwards, and the absence of sound becomes part of the record itself, but this is not the calm after a storm. We are in its eye. It looms large above our heads. *Kollaps* annunciates an inevitable transformation in music. In these final moments of silence, Einstürzende Neubauten is born from its own ashes.

Epilogue
Alles in Allem

If the world had indeed come to an end sometime in the early 1980s, as Einstürzende Neubauten so vehemently proclaimed, *Kollaps* might have been a last burst of energy, a furious celebration of life and love at the brink of annihilation, a final goodbye. Together with everything else, it might even have been the end of music itself. But the world did not end in 1981 or in 1984, not in 1990 or 1997, not in 2001 or 2012 or even in 2020. It just continued. And so did the band.

In October and November 1981, Einstürzende Neubauten joined the *Berliner Krankheit* (Berliner Sickness) tour of West Germany, together with Sprung aus den Wolken and Mekanik Destruektiw Komandoe. It left the band members frustrated with the state of their home country, so in 1982, they played over twenty shows throughout the rest of Western Europe.

Over the course of the 1980s, the line-up of Bargeld, Unruh, Einheit, Chung and Hacke inadvertently became a streamlined live act. They recorded four more albums together, building and expanding upon the musical and lyrical themes they began to explore on *Kollaps*. *½ Mensch* (1985) even contains another version of 'Sehnsucht', and in 1987, they revisited a song that first appeared on *Stahlmusik* and epitomized their fundamental attitude: 'Kein Bestandteil Sein' (To Be No Part of It).

By 1989, Einstürzende Neubauten had become a household name. Their fifth album, *Haus der Lüge* (House of Lies), was released two months before the collapse of the Berlin Wall in November 1989. This announced the disappearance of West-Berlin and the emergence of a reunited Germany. Some years later, Marc Chung and F.M. Einheit left the band, leaving Bargeld, Unruh and Hacke to finish the aptly titled *Ende Neu* (Ending New, 1996) as a trio.

At the brink of the new millennium, Jochen Arbeit and Rudolf Moser joined the band, and the album *Silence Is Sexy* (2000) once again confronted the tumultuous history of Berlin, now again the capital of all of Germany. Starting with *Perpetuum Mobile* (2004), the band's albums have been funded by their most loyal fans. This online 'Supporter's Project' made them completely independent from record labels.

Back in 1981, few people would have guessed that Einstürzende Neubauten would ever celebrate their tenth, let alone their fortieth, anniversary. Still, this is exactly what they did with the release of *Alles in Allem* (All in All) in 2020. At its core, the nucleus of Bargeld and Unruh is still active.

All this time, *Kollaps* remained an indestructible force.

'We had a thousand ideas / and all were good.'[1]

Einstürzende Neubauten discography

Pre-dating Einstürzende Neubauten

Köster/Bargeld and N·Dih/Blixa/Susä. *Einstürzende Neubauten*. Eisengrau, 1980, cassette.

Early work

Live in Kunstkopfstereo. Eisengrau. May 1980, cassette.
Chaos → Sehnsucht/Energie. Eisengrau. June 1980, cassette.
Stahlmusik. Eisengrau 1002. June 1980, cassette.
Fuer den Untergang Monogam 005. September 1980, 7″ vinyl single.
- Side A included on *Kalte Sterne: Early Recordings*, 2004.
- Side B included on *Strategies Against Architecture 80-83*, 1984.

Various artists. *Monogam Sampler*. Monogram 006. February 1981, vinyl LP.
- Six songs on side B are credited to Einstürzende Neubauten & Die Sentimentale Jugend (pseudonym of Alexander Hacke). Three of these are included on *Kalte Sterne: Early Recordings*, 2004.

Various artists. *Lieber Zuviel als Zuwenig (ZickZack Sommerhits 81)*. Zickzack ZZ45, June 1981, vinyl LP.

– Contains the song 'Bakterien für Eure Seele', also included on *Kalte Sterne: Early Recordings*, 2004.

Kalte Sterne. Zickzack ZZ40. July 1981, 2 x 7" vinyl single.

– Included on *Kalte Sterne: Early Recordings*, 2004.

Kollaps. Zickzack ZZ65, 5 October 1981, vinyl LP.

– Reissue: Potomak 2517-2. 2002, CD.

Thirsty Animal. Self-released. 1982, 12" vinyl single.

– Side A featuring Lydia Lunch and Roland S. Howard. Included on *Kalte Sterne: Early Recordings*, 2004.

Stahldubversions. Eisengrau/Rip off Rip 6. 1982, cassette.

– Included on *Kollaps* CD reissue, 2002.

Various artists. *Bandsalat*. Good Noise VGNS. 1982, vinyl LP.

– Contains 'Tan-tze-Dub', also included (as 'Tan-Ze-Dub') on *Kalte Sterne: Early Recordings*, 2004.

Subsequent studio albums

Zeichnungen des Patienten O.T. Some Bizzare SBVART 2. 1983, vinyl LP.

– Reissue: Potomak 25172. 2002, CD.

½ Mensch. Some Bizzare Bart 331. 1985, vinyl LP.

– Reissue: Potomak 26142. 2002, CD.

Fuenf auf der Nach Oben Offenen Richterskala. Some Bizzare Bart 332. 1987, vinyl LP.

– Reissue: Potomak 26502. 2002, CD.

Haus der Luege. Some Bizzare Bart 333. 1989, vinyl LP.
- Reissue: Potomak 20002. 2002, CD.

Tabula Rasa. Mute BETON 106. 1993, CD.

Ende Neu. Mute BETON 504. 1996, CD.
- Reissue: Potomak 919822. 2009, CD.

Silence Is Sexy. Mute CDSTUMM182. 2000, CD.
- Reissue: Potomak 957052. 2011, CD.

Perpetuum Mobile. Mute CDSTUMM221. 2004, CD.

Grundstück. Potomak Neubauten-2CD. 2005, CD.
- Reissue: Potomak 158682. 2018, CD.

Alles Wieder Offen. Potomak 2007/9. 2007, CD.

Jewels. Potomak 919782. 2008, CD.

Lament. BMG 538013752. 2014, CD.

Alles in Allem. Potomak 195992. 2020, CD.

Rampen (apm: Alien Pop Music). Potomak. 254752. 2024, CD.

Compilations

Strategies Against Architecture 80-83. Mute STUMM14. 1984, vinyl LP.
- Reissue: Mute STUMM14. 1988, CD.

Strategies Against Architecture II. Mute 61100-2. 1991, 2 x CD.

Strategies Against Architecture III. Potomak RTD 100.0003.2. 2001, 2 x CD

Kalte Sterne: Early Recordings. Mute CDSTUMM137. CD, 2004.

Strategies Against Architecture IV. Mute CDSTUMM325. 2 x CD, 2010.

Greatest Hits. Potomak CD 133952. CD, 2016.

Acknowledgements

This book finds its origin in what seems to be a different time and place. Some ten years before we finalized the manuscript, the idea to write about Einstürzende Neubauten's debut album was borne from the debris of our musicology studies. We studied in different cities in the Netherlands – separated, though, by a train ride of less than half an hour – but shared the same disgruntled professor who taught at both universities and was dissatisfied with the discipline. He introduced us to one another as well as to a more philosophical approach towards music. Soon after, we discovered our shared musical interests in general and our predilection for Einstürzende Neubauten in particular. Ideas for this book have been gestating ever since.

In the intermittent years, failed attempts, other books, projects and life in general intervened, but we still regularly returned to *Kollaps*: working on a proposal, exchanging ideas, talking about the music, attending concerts. It never really left us. Luckily, therefore, the project ultimately found a welcome home with Bloomsbury's 33⅓ Europe series. We owe much thanks to editor Leah Babb-Rosenfeld and series editor Fabian Holt for offering us this chance and for their patience. Thanks as well to Rachel Moore and everyone else at Bloomsbury for supporting the writing process.

Other people we would like to thank are Ruben Braeken and Florian de Backere for their helpful commentary on an early draft; Tom Klaassen for making his first pressing of *Kollaps*, including the original booklet, available; Arthur Benschop for his cunning advice that freed up time and space to write this book; Koen Damhuis for his French; and Rosanne and Doris for putting up with late writing hours and the occasional absent-mindedness.

Acknowledgements

Notes

Prologue

1 Much of the information on dates and details of releases and concerts, here and throughout the book, is based on the sections on Einstürzende Neubauten at *From the Archives*: https://www.fromthearchives.com.

2 All references to releases by Einstürzende Neubauten are listed in the Einstürzende Neubauten Discography.

3 Cited from the booklet accompanying *Kollaps*. All translations of otherwise untranslated sources are our own.

4 Bargeld in Klaus Maeck, ed., *Hör mit Schmerzen/Listen with Pain: Einstürzende Neubauten 1980-1996*, rev. ed. (Berlin: Gestalten Verlag, 1996), 20.

5 Bargeld in Kenneth Laddish and Mark Dippé, 'Blixa Einstuerzende: Bargeld Harassed', *Mondo 2000*, 1993. https://seelebrenntarchive.wordpress.com/2013/04/17/bargeld-harassed-interview-1993.

Steh auf Berlin

1 Bargeld in Jürgen Teipel, *Verschwende Deine Jugend*, rev. ed. (Berlin: Suhrkamp, 2012), 331.

2 Ibid., 332.

3 Bargeld in Shryane, *Blixa Bargeld and Einstürzende Neubauten: German Experimental Music. 'Evading do-re-mi'* (Burlington: Ashgate, 2011), 4.

4 Bargeld in Teipel, *Verschwende,* 291. This imagery of 'scarred terrain' is also a central motif in the song 'Die Befindlichkeit des Landes' (The Lay of the Land) on *Silence Is Sexy* (2000), which thematizes the rapid changes in Berlin's cityscape after the fall of the wall in 1989.

5 Walter Benjamin, 'On the Concept of History', trans. Harry Zohn, in *Selected Writings Volume 4, 1938–1940*, ed. Howard Eiland and Michael W. Jennings (Cambridge, MA: The Belknap Press of Harvard University Press, 2006), 392. The angel of history explicitly appears in 'Die Befindlichkeit des Landes' (*Silence Is Sexy*, 2000): 'Hängt sie mit ausgebreiteten Schwingen / Ohne Schlaf, und starren Blicks / In richtung Trümmer / Hinter ihr die Zukunft aufgetürmt' (She hangs with widespread wings / sleepless and with frozen gaze / pointed at rubble / behind her the future piling up).

6 Mirko M. Hall, *Musical Revolutions in German Culture. Musicking against the Grain, 1800–1980* (New York: Palgrave Macmillan, 2014), 117–118.

7 Unruh in Max Dax and Robert Defcon, *Einstürzende Neubauten. No Beauty Without Danger*, trans. Margit Sander and Alexander Paulick (Bremen: Druckhaus Hamburg, 2005), 94.

8 Hacke in Ibid., 15.

9 Ibid.

10 Bargeld in Maeck, *Hör*, 33.

11 Klaus Laufer (pseudonym of Wolfgang Müller) in Ibid., 18.

12 *Stahlmusik* was released on cassette by Bargeld's Eisengrau label in October 1980. A second edition appeared in 1981, but it has not been officially re-released since.

13 'Tanze, tanze, tanze den Untergang / Energie stürzt ein'.

14 *Strategies Against Architecture 80–83* (1984) lists the song under its subtitle 'Krieg in den Städten' (War in the Cities).

15 Luigi Russolo, *The Art of Noise (Futurist Manifesto 1913)*, trans. Robert Filliou (New York: Something Else Press, 1967), 5.

16 Bargeld in S. Alexander Reed, *Assimilate. A Critical History of Industrial Music* (New York: Oxford University Press, 2013), 87.

17 'Hinlegen / Verbrannte Erde'.

18 'Ich stehe auf Feuer / Ich stehe auf Rauch / Ich stehe auf Krach / Und ich stehe auf Steine'.

19 'Ich stehe auf Krankheit / Ich stehe auf Niedergang / Ich stehe auf Ende'.

20 Bargeld in Maeck, *Hör*, 41.

21 Chris Bohn in Ibid., 51.

Kollaps

1 Blixa Bargeld, *Stimme frißt Feuer* (Berlin: Merve Verlag, 1988), 98.

2 Ibid., 101.

3 Ibid., 98.

4 Wolfgang Müller, ed., *Geniale Dilletanten* (Berlin: Merve Verlag, 1982), 10.

5 Einheit in Teipel, *Verschwende*, 378.

6 Bargeld in Andrea Cangioli, *Einstürzende Neubauten* (Rome: Stampa Alternativa, 1993), 14.

7 Müller, *Geniale Dilletanten*.

8 See, for instance, the catalogue from a retrospective exhibition in Haus der Kunst in München in 2015: Leonhard Emmerling and Mathilde Weh, eds, *Geniale Dilletanten. Subkultur der 1980er-Jahre in Deutschland* (Berlin: Hatje Cantz, 2015).

9 Bargeld included the second Ton Steine Scherben album, *Keine Macht für Niemand*, in a list of 'records that changed his life'. Bargeld in Thomas Clausen, '5 Records that Changed My Life: Blixa Bargeld', in *Sonic Seducer. Einstürzende Neubauten Chronik*, ed. Kai Reinbold and Thomas Abresche (Berlin: Thomas Vogel Media, 2017), 137–8. Ton Steine Scherben, *Keine Macht für Niemand*, David Volksmund Produktion, 1972, 2 x vinyl LP.

10 Bargeld in Laddish and Dippé, 'Blixa'.

11 Gut in Dax and Defcon, *Einstürzende Neubauten*, 48.

12 Ibid., 19.

13 Bargeld in Teipel, *Verschwende*, 82.

14 Richard Huelsenbeck, 'Introduction', in *Dada Almanac*, ed. Malcolm Green, trans. Derk Wynand (London: Atlas Press, 1993), 9.

15 Einstürzende Neubauten paid homage to Dada with 'Let's Do It a Dada' (*Alles Wieder Offen*, 2007).

16 Din A Testbild, *Abfall Garbage/Glas Konkav*, self-released. 1979, 7" vinyl single.

17 Huelsenbeck, 'Introduction', 13.

18 Blixa Bargeld, *Headcleaner, Text für Einstürzende Neubauten/ Text for Collapsing New Buildings*, trans. Finbarr Morrin, ed. Maria Zinfert (Hamburg: Musikverlage, 1997), 160.

19 Bargeld in Maeck, *Hör*, 33. Other terms they used are 'contemporary German folk music' and 'hard core new age'. Laddish and Dippé, 'Blixa'.

20 Forty years later, in 2020, Bargeld acknowledged as much when he sang of the band's heyday: 'Wir hatten tausend Ideen, und alle war'n gut'. (We had a thousand ideas / And all were good) ('Am Landwehrkanal', *Alles in Allem*, 2020).

Tanz Debil

1 Bargeld in Maeck, *Hör*, 20.

2 Bettina Köster in Teipel, *Verschwende*, 190. On 'Susej' (*Alles Wieder Offen*, 2007) Bargeld looked back on his former self and sang: 'Ausgezehrt und abgemergelt/Wie in der erinnerung' (Haggard and emaciated/as recollected).

3 Nick Cave in Daniel Dylan Wray, '"They'd Greet us with Fire Extinguishers!": The Wild Times of Blixa Bargeld', *The Guardian*, 18 May 2020, www.theguardian.com.

4 Unruh in Teipel, *Verschwende*, 191.

5 Dax and Defcon, *Einstürzende Neubauten*, 70.

6 Chung in Ibid., 69.

7 Bargeld, *Stimme*, 101.

8 Bargeld in Maeck, *Hör*, 51.

9 Bartel and Gut continued to perform with their punk-jazz band Mania D., founded in 1979. In 1981, Mania D.

evolved into experimental electronic band Malaria! and subsequently into Matador.

10   Bargeld in Dax and Defcon, *Einstürzende Neubauten*, 61–2.

11   Bargeld, *Stimme*,101.

12   'Sehnsucht / Kommt aus dem Chaos / Sehnsucht / Ist die einzige Energie.'

13   The equation first appeared as the title of Einstürzende Neubauten's second cassette: a collection of live recordings featuring roughly the same line-up as *Live in Kunstkopfstereo*. It was released on Eisengrau in an edition of twenty copies in June 1980.

14   Bargeld in Dax and Defcon, *Einstürzende Neubauten*, 12.

15   Bargeld in Max Dax, 'Jede Narbe erinnert an ein Konzert', *Die Welt*, 27 March 2005, www.welt.de. Also see Dax and Defcon, *Einstürzende Neubauten*, 85.

16   Hacke in Ibid., 80.

17   Graphic designer and photographer Fritz Brinckmann remembered: 'At the time, Blixa was a man of the absolute present. There was no yesterday or tomorrow. Not even the previous minute or the next minute mattered – just the absolute now.' Brinckmann in Ibid., 10.

18   Daniel Chua and Alexander Rehding, *Alien Listening: Voyager's Golden Record and Music from Earth* (New York: Zone Books, 2021), 191. Emphasis in original.

19   Bargeld in Maeck, *Hör*, 20.

Schmerzen Hören

1   Einheit in Dax and Defcon, *Einstürzende Neubauten*, 41.

2 Moland Fengkov and Sandrine Marques, 'Interview de Alexander Hacke - Einstürzende Neubauten', *La Plume Noire*, 2005. http://www.plume-noire.com/interviews/musique/alexanderhacke.html.

3 Bargeld, *Stimme*, 19–20.

4 Mutternacht, 'Einstürzende Neubauten - Kollaps [Live]', youtube.com, 2 January 2010. https://youtu.be/Hkrv0Q11tWM.

5 Bargeld in Chris Bohn, 'Let's Hear it for the Untergang Show', *New Musical Express*, 5 February 1983, 23.

6 Gut in Wolfgang Müller, *Subkultur Westberlin 1979–1989* (Hamburg: Philo Fine Arts, 2013), 176.

7 Bargeld in Dax and Defcon, *Einstürzende Neubauten*, 7. Incidentally, the male variant of Blixa, 'Blixer', appears in the liner notes of the *Monogam Sampler*, issued a year before the release of *Kollaps* in October 1980.

8 Kunstmull, 'SevenScrewsNonbinary', in Blixa Bargeld, *Phase IV* (Berlin: Potomak, 2020), 24–25. On 'Seven Screws' (*Alles in Allem*, 2020), Bargeld sings: 'I draw myself anew/non-binary I: forever new'.

9 Einheit in Dax and Defcon, *Einstürzende Neubauten*, 80–1.

10 Antonin Artaud, *Watchfiends & Rack Screams: Works from the Final Period*, trans. Clayton Eshleman and Bernard Bador (Boston: Exact Change, 1995), 307.

11 'Stell dich tot / Stell dich tot / Gier! / Stell dich tot / Gier! / Öffne meine Venen / Dicht unter der Haut'.

12 'U-Haft' stands for *Untersuchungshaft*, meaning custody. 'Muzak' was originally the name of an American company selling background music, but the word has come to refer to bland, generic music in general.

13 Unruh in Shryane, *Blixa Bargeld*, 185.

14 Roland Barthes, 'The Grain of the Voice', in *Image Music Text*, trans. and ed. Stephen Heat (London: Fontana Press, 1977), 179–89.

15 'Wir zerstören die Städte'.

16 Bargeld in Shryane, *Blixa Bargeld*, 3.

17 Bargeld in Bohn, 'Untergang Show', 23.

Draussen ist Feindlich

1 'Einstürzende Neubauten. (Berlin 1st April 1980– present). Discography (I) (1980–1997)', From the Archives, last modified 30 September 2015. https://www .fromthearchives.org/en/discography1.html. Beate Bartel in fact recalls that the line-up of 'Blixa, Andrew, Bettina and Susä [was] already called Einstürzende Neubauten' back in 1979. Bartel in Dax and Defcon, *Einstürzende Neubauten*, 21. However, the booklet accompanying the first pressings of *Kollaps* calls it a 'precursor-formation' (*Vorläufer-formation*) and lists 'Einstürzende Neubauten' as the title of the cassette.

2 Before Bargeld took over, the Eisengrau shop was run by Bettina Köster and Gudrun Gut, who founded it in 1979. NU had a workshop in the cellar. Teipel, *Verschwende*, 190–1; Dax and Defcon, *Einstürzende Neubauten*, 26–7.

3 This version later appears as 'Tan-tze-Dub' on a compilation album called *Bandsalat* (1982) and as 'Tan-Ze-Dub' on *Kalte Sterne: Early Recording*s (2004).

4 Laufer (pseudonym of Wolfgang Müller) in Maeck, *Hör*, 18.

5 Unruh in *Einstürzende Neubauten – Seele Brennt*, DVD, directed by Christian Beetz and Birgit Herdlitschke, 2000 (Berlin: Neue Visionen, 2005). Bargeld remembers things differently: according to him, the engineer left because the label only paid for the studio. Bargeld in Dax and Defcon, *Einstürzende Neubauten*, 68.

6 Einheit in Beetz and Herdlitschke, *Einstürzende Neubauten*, 2005.

7 'Geh nicht weg / Nie wieder / Halt mich fest / Ich halt dich fest'.

8 Einheit in Maeck, *Hör*, 24. Hans Rosenthal (1925–87) was a popular German radio and television host of Jewish origin. Ronald Reagan (1911–2004) was an American actor, who served as the fortieth president of the United States from 1981 to 1989.

9 Bargeld, *Stimme*, 98; translation from Hall, *Musical Revolutions*, 130.

10 David Toop, 'Replicant: On Dub', in *Audio Culture: Readings in Modern Music*, ed. Christoph Cox and Daniel Warner (New York: Continuum Group, 2004), 356.

11 According to Hacke, Bargeld 'had an incredible collection of reggae records. He mainly collected reggae singles, where there wouldn't be any words in the title. Singles that had titles like 'Wagga-dagga-da' or something like that. He thought that was great. Every time I visited him he had a new single: 'listen to this – the chorus goes "whoappa, whoappa, whoappa . . . ! Blixa used to listen to a lot of reggae"'. Hacke in Dax and Defcon, *Einstürzende Neubauten*, 19.

12 *Stahldubversions* was originally released on cassette on Eisengrau in 1982 and included on the 2003 CD reissue of *Kollaps*.

13 Toop, 'Replicant', 356.

14 'Schliess dich ein mit mir / Hier sind wir sicher' ('Draussen ist Feindlich').

Negativ Nein

1 Einheit in Kirsten Borchardt, *Einstürzende Neubauten* (Höfen: Hannibal, 2003), 68. Unruh in Dax and Defcon, *Einstürzende Neubauten*, 70. 'Kollaps. Einstürzende Neubauten. 1981', 1001 Random Album Generator. https://1001albumsgenerator.com/albums/5ESlb1RVMYf hixc1x8JRts/kollaps (accessed 26 November 2023).

2 Unruh in Dax and Defcon, *Einstürzende Neubauten*, 70.

3 Ibid; Lou Reed, *Metal Machine Music (The Amine β Ring)*, RCA CPL2-1101, 1975, 2 x vinyl LP.

4 Bargeld in Teipel, *Verschwende*, 288.

5 Ibid.

6 Bargeld in Maeck, *Hör*, 38.

7 'Das Lied schläft in der Maschine', from 'NNNAAAMMM' (*Ende Neu/Ending New*, 1996).

8 In thermodynamics, information theory and cybernetics, this tension is formalized as the interplay between entropy (disorder and randomness) and negentropy (order and control).

9 Bargeld in Maeck, *Hör*, 20.

10   'Negativ Nein', liner notes for *Strategies Against Architecture 80–83* (1984).

11   Michel Serres, *The Parasite*, trans. Lawrence R. Schehr (Baltimore: John Hopkins University Press, 1982), 126.

Jet'm

1   Bargeld in Laddish and Dippé, 'Blixa'.

2   Jane Birkin and Serge Gainsbourg, 'Je T'aime. . . Moi Non Plus'. Fontana TF 1042, 1969, 7" vinyl single.

3   'Scorning instead of moaning', writes Thomas Pilgrim. Pilgrim, 'Rezension. Einstürzende Neubauten "Kollaps"', in Reinbold and Abresche, *Sonic Seducer*, 18. Kirsten Borchardt notes the 'corny synthesiser' sound and suggests the band 'self-evidently' excluded the erotic atmosphere. Borchardt, *Einstürzende Neubauten*, 70.

4   Walter Benjamin, 'Karl Kraus', trans. Edmund Jeph in *Selected Writings Volume 2, 1927–1934*, ed. Michael W. Jennings, Howard Eiland and Gary Smith (Cambridge, MA: The Belknap Press of Harvard University, 1999), 454.

5   Bargeld in Laddish and Dippé, 'Blixa'.

6   Benjamin, 'Karl Kraus', 455.

7   Walter Benjamin, 'One-Way Street', in *Selected Writings, Volume 1, 1913–1926*, ed. Marcus Bullock and Michael W. Junnings, trans. Edmund Jephcott (Cambridge, MA: The Belknap Press of Harvard University Press, 1996), 481.

8   'Verbrenne mich, / Reiß mich nieder, nieder, immer wieder'.

9   Jean Jenkins, ed., *Ethiopia Vol 2: Music of the Desert Nomads*, Tangent Records, 1970, vinyl record.

10 The song 'Vorm Krieg' is a case in point. Some twenty seconds long, it is a collage made of the wind section from Barney Bigard Sextet recording of 'Sweet Marijuana Brown' from 1945, with Art Tatum on piano. 'Vorm Krieg' is like a beam of light that falls through the crack of the door. It is overflowing with musical potential. Barney Bigard Sextet, *Sweet Marijuana Brown/Blues for Art's Sake*, Black & White 13, 1945, 10" shellac record.

11 Bargeld in Clausen, '5 Records', 138.

12 Bargeld in Laddish and Dippé, 'Blixa'.

13 Walter Benjamin, 'The Destructive Character', in *Selected Writings Volume 2*, 541.

14 Fittingly, the German title of Einstürzende Neubauten's monograph celebrating their twenty-five-year jubilee is *Nur was nicht ist, ist möglich*, from the song 'Was ist ist' (*Ende Neu*, 1996). Only what is not, is possible: to reach that which is not, one needs to break through what already exists. This comes with a price, though: sometimes, things get broken. As the English translation of the book exemplifies: *No Beauty Without Danger* (from 'Keine Schönheit (ohne Gefahr)', *Fünf auf der nach oben Offenen Richterskala*, 1987). Dax and Defcon, *Einstürzende Neubauten*.

Sehnsucht

1 According to sources in the band, Helga is the name of Unruh's mother.

2 As Benjamin writes: 'In jazz, noise is emancipated. Jazz appears at a moment when, increasingly, noise is eliminated from the process of production, of traffic, and of commerce. Likewise in radio.' Walter Benjamin, *The Arcades Project*, trans. Howard Eiland and Kevin McLaughlin (Cambridge, MA: The Belknap Press of Harvard, 2002), 862.

3 Barney Bigard Sextet, *Sweet Marijuana Brown/Blues for Art's Sake*.

4 'Kollaps / Unsre Irrfahrten / Zerstören die Städte / Und nächtliches Wandern / Macht sie dem Erdboden gleich'.

5 'Und immer fragt der Seufzer, wo? / Im Geisterhauch tönt's mir zurück: / Dort, wo du nicht bist, dort ist das Glück'. Schubert, Franz. 'Der Wanderer'. This is Franz Schubert's *Der Wanderer*, numbered D489 in his catalogue, which uses Georg Philipp Schmidt von Lübeck's poem *Des Fremdlings Abendlied* (1821). Schubert also wrote another Lied called *Der Wanderer* (D649), on a poem by Friedrich Schlegel. Franz Schubert, 'Der Wanderer', in *Schubert Lieder-album, Band 1, Schöne Müllerin - Winterreise - Schwanengesang und 32 ausgewählte Lieder. Ausgabe für mittlere Stimme*, ed. L. Benda (Braunschweig: Henry Litolff's Verlag, ca. 1914).

6 'Sehnsucht / Sehnsucht / Kommt aus dem Chaos / Sehnsucht / Sehnsucht / Ist die einzige Energie / Meine Sehnsucht / Meine Sucht / Sehnsucht / Ist die einzige Energie'.

7 The *Deutsches Wörterbuch* (German dictionary), started in the nineteenth century by the brothers Grimm, connects the words *Sucht* and *Suchten* with *Seufzer*, which in the Low German dialect means an audible sigh. Jacob Grimm and Wilhelm Grimm, 'Sucht, f. bis Süchteln', in *Deutsches Wörterbuch von Jacob Grimm und Wilhelm Grimm*, digitized version on Wörterbuchnetz, version 01/23 (Trier: Trier Center for Digital Humanities). https://www.woerterbuchnetz.de/DWB (accessed 8 August 2023).

Incidentally, the Dutch equivalent *zucht* also means 'sigh', as well as an urge, more often than not also bordering on obsession.

8 Cf. desire as discussed in Spinoza's *Ethics*: 'Desire is man's very essence, insofar as it is conceived to be determined, from any given affection of it, to do something.' And the essence of something, according to Spinoza is 'the striving by which each thing strives to persevere in its being is nothing but the actual essence of the thing'. Desire, thus, is a perpetual force that governs life. Benedict de Spinoza, *Ethics*, trans. and ed. Edwin Curley (London: Penguin books, 1996), 104 and 75.

9 As a sickness, *Sehnsucht* might even be called an inflammation: a spark that lights a raging, all-consuming fire. Fire would become an important theme in the work of Einstürzende Neubauten, for instance in the songs 'Abfackeln' (*Zeichnungen des Patienten O. T.*, 1983) and 'Feurio!' (*Haus der Lüge*, 1989).

10 The track 'Valium', recorded during Einstürzende Neubauten's first concert on 1 April 1980 and released on their second cassette, *Chaos → Sehnsucht/Energie. Eisengrau* (1980), consists of the band playing around with a recording of gamelan music.

11 'Der Beweis meines positiven Denkens ist Deine Geburt!!!'.

Epilogue

1 'Wir hatten tausend Ideen, und alle war'n gut' ('Am Landwehrkanal', *Alles in Allem*, 2020).

References

Bibliography

1001 Random Album Generator. 'Kollaps. Einstürzende
Neubauten'. 1981. https://1001albumsgenerator.com/albums
/5ESlb1RVMYfhixc1x8JRts/kollaps (accessed 26 November
2023).

Artaud, Antonin. *The Theatre and its Double*. New York: Grove
Press, 1958.

Artaud, Antonin. *Watchfiends & Rack Screams: Works from the Final
Period*. Translated by Clayton Eshleman and Bernard Bador.
Boston: Exact Change, 1995.

Bargeld, Blixa. *Headcleaner. Text für Einstürzende Neubauten/
Text for Collapsing New Buildings*. Edited by Maria Zinfert.
Translated by Finbarr Morrin and Matthew Partridge.
Hamburg: Musikverlage, 1997.

Bargeld, Blixa. *Stimme frißt Feuer*. Berlin: Merve Verlag, 1988.

Barthes, Roland. 'The Grain of the Voice'. In *Image Music Text*,
translated and edited by Stephen Heat, 179–89. London:
Fontana Press, 1977.

Benjamin, Walter. *The Arcades Project*. Translated by Howard
Eiland and Kevin McLaughlin. Cambridge, MA: The Belknap
Press of Harvard University Press, 2002.

Benjamin, Walter. 'The Destructive Character'. Translated by
Edmund Jephcott. In *Selected Writings Volume 2, 1927-1934*,
edited by Michael W. Jennings, Howard Eiland and Gary

Smith, 541–2. Cambridge, MA: The Belknap Press of Harvard University Press, 1999.

Benjamin, Walter. 'Karl Kraus'. Translated by Edmund Jephcott. In *Selected Writings Volume 2, 1927-1934*, edited by Michael W. Jennings, Howard Eiland and Gary Smith, 433–58. Cambridge, MA: The Belknap Press of Harvard University Press, 1999.

Benjamin, Walter. 'One-way Street'. Translated by Edmund Jephcott. In *Selected Writings, Volume 1, 1913-1926*, edited by Marcus Bullock and Michael W. Jennings, 444–88. Cambridge, MA: The Belknap Press of Harvard University Press, 1996.

Benjamin, Walter. 'On the Concept of History'. Translated by Harry Zohn. In *Selected Writings Volume 4, 1938-1940*, edited by Howard Eiland and Michael W. Jennings, 389–400. Cambridge, MA: The Belknap Press of Harvard University Press, 2006.

Bohn, Chris. 'Let's Hear it for the Untergang Show'. *New Musical Express* 22–23 (5 February 1983): 34.

Borchardt, Kirsten. *Einstürzende Neubauten*. Höfen: Hannibal, 2003.

Cangioli, Andrea, *Einstürzende Neubauten*. Rome: Stampa Alternativa, 1993.

Chua, Daniel and Alexander Rehding. *Alien Listening: Voyager's Golden Record and Music from Earth*. New York: Zone Books, 2021.

Clausen, Thomas. '5 Records that Changed My Life: Blixa Bargeld'. In *Sonic Seducer. Einstürzende Neubauten. Chronik*, edited by Kai Reinbold and Thomas Abresche, 137–8. Berlin: Thomas Vogel Media, 2017.

Dax, Max. 'Jede Narbe erinnert an ein Konzert'. *Die Welt*, 27 March 2005, www.welt.de.

Dax, Max and Robert Defcon. *Einstürzende Neubauten. No Beauty Without Danger*. Translated by Margit Sander and Alexander Paulick. Bremen: Druckhaus Hamburg, 2005.

Emmerling, Leonhard and Mathilde Weh, eds. *Geniale Dilletanten. Subkultur der 1980er-Jahre in Deutschland*. Berlin: Hatje Cantz, 2015. Published following the exhibition *'Geniale Dilletanten.' Subkultur der* 1980er-*Jahre in Deutschland* at Haus der Kunst, München.

Fengkov, Moland and Sandrine Marques. 'Interview de Alexander Hacke - Einstürzende Neubauten'. *La Plume Noire*, 2005. http://www.plume-noire.com/interviews/musique/alexanderhacke.html.

From The Archives. 'Einstürzende Neubauten. (Berlin 1st April 1980 - now). Discography (I) (1980–1997)'. Last modified 30 September 2015. https://www.fromthearchives.org/en/discography1.html.

Grimm, Jacob and Wilhelm Grimm. 'Sucht, f. bis Süchteln'. In *Deutsches Wörterbuch von Jacob Grimm und Wilhelm Grimm*. Digitised version on Wörterbuchnetz, Version 01/23. Trier: Center for Digital Humanities. https://www.woerterbuchnetz.de/DWB (accessed 8 August 2023).

Hall, Mirko M. *Musical Revolutions in German Culture. Musicking against the Grain, 1800–1980*. New York: Palgrave Macmillan, 2014.

Huelsenbeck, Richard. 'Introduction'. In *Dada Almanac*, translated by Derk Wynand. Edited by Malcolm Green, 9–14. London: Atlas Press, 1993.

Kunstmull. 'SevenScrewsNonbinary'. In *Phase IV*, edited by Blixa Bargeld, 24–5. Berlin: Potomak, 2020.

Laddish, Kenneth and Mark Dippé. 'Blixa Einstuerzende: Bargeld Harassed'. *Mondo 2000*, 1993. https://seelebrenntarchive.wordpress.com/2013/04/17/bargeld-harassed-interview-1993.

Maeck, Klaus, ed. *Hör mit Schmerzen/Listen with Pain: Einstürzende Neubauten 1980–1996*. Rev. ed. Berlin: Gestalten Verlag, 1996.

Müller, Wolfgang, ed. *Geniale Dilletanten*. Berlin: Merve Verlag, 1982.

Müller, Wolfgang. *Subkultur Westberlin 1979–1989*. Hamburg: Philo Fine Arts, 2013.

Pilgrim, Thomas. 'Rezension. Einstürzende Neubauten "Kollaps"'. In *Sonic Seducer. Einstürzende Neubauten. Chronik*, edited by Kai Reinbold and Thomas Abresche, 18–19. Berlin: Thomas Vogel Media, 2017.

Reed, S. Alexander. *Assimilate. A Critical History of Industrial Music*. New York: Oxford University Press, 2013.

Russolo, Luigi. *The Art of Noise. Futurist Manifesto 1913*. Translated by Robert Filliou. New York: Something Else Press, 1967.

Schubert, Franz. 'Der Wanderer'. In *Schubert Lieder-Album. Band 1. Schöne Müllerin. Winterreise. Schwanengesang und 32 ausgewählte Lieder. Ausgabe für mittlere Stimme. (Mezzo-Sopran oder Bariton.)*, edited by L. Benda, 193–5. Braunschweig: Henry Litolff's Verlag, 1914.

Serres, Michel. *The Parasite*. Translated by Lawrence R. Schehr. Baltimore: John Hopkins University Press, 1982.

Shryane, Jennifer. *Blixa Bargeld and Einstürzende Neubauten: German Experimental Music. 'Evading do-re-mi'*. Burlington: Ashgate, 2011.

Spinoza, Benedict de. *Ethics*. Translated and edited by Edwin Curley. London: Penguin Books, 1996.

Teipel, Jürgen. *Verschwende Deine Jugend*. Rev. ed. Berlin: Suhrkamp, 2012.

Toop, David. 'Replicant: On Dub'. In *Audio Culture: Readings in Modern Music*, edited by Christoph Cox and Daniel Warner, 355–7. New York: Continuum Group, 2004.

Wray, Daniel Dylan. '"They'd Greet us with Fire Extinguishers!": The Wild Times of Blixa Bargeld'. *The Guardian*, 18 May 2020, www .theguardian.com.

Discography

All releases by Einstürzende Neubauten are listed in the separate Einstürzende Neubauten Discography.

Barney Bigard Sextet. *Sweet Marijuana Brown / Blues for Art's Sake.* Black & White 13. 1945, 10" shellac record.

Birkin, Jane and Serge Gainsbourg. *Je T'aime . . . Moi Non Plus.* Fontana TF 1042, 1969, 7" vinyl single.

Din A Testbild. *Abfall Garbage / Glas Konkav.* Self-released, 1979, 7" vinyl single.

Jenkins, Jean, ed. *Ethiopia Vol 2: Music of the Desert Nomads.* Tangent Records, 1970, vinyl LP.

Reed, Lou. *Metal Machine Music (The Amine β Ring).* RCA CPL2-1101, 1975, 2 x vinyl LP.

Ton Steine Scherben. *Keine Macht für Niemand.* David Volksmund Produktion, 1972, 2 x vinyl LP.

Videography

Einstürzende Neubauten – Seele Brennt. Directed by Christian Beetz and Birgit Herdlitschke, 2000. Berlin: Neue Visionen, 2005, DVD.

Mutternacht. 'Einstürzende Neubauten - Kollaps [Live]'. *Youtube .com*, 2 January 2010. https://youtu.be/Hkrv0Q11tWM.

Index

Note: Page locators followed by 'n' refer to notes.